The Small Business Finance Raiser

Building Your Business
Other titles in the series are:

See back of book for details

The Small Business Finance Raiser

Stan Mason

Business Books
London Melbourne Sydney Auckland Johannesburg

Business Books Ltd

An imprint of Century Hutchinson Ltd

Brookmount House, 62–65 Chandos Place, London, WC2N 4NW

Hutchinson Publishing Group (Australia) Pty Ltd
16–22 Church Street, Hawthorn, Melbourne, Victoria 3122

Hutchinson Group (NZ) Ltd
32–34 View Road, PO Box 40–086, Glenfield, Auckland 10

Hutchinson Group (SA) (Pty) Ltd
PO Box 337, Bergvlei 2012, South Africa

First published 1985
© Stan Mason 1985
Reprinted 1986

Set in Helvetica by Words & Pictures Ltd,
Thornton Heath, Surrey

Printed and bound in Great Britain by
Anchor Brendon Ltd, Tiptree, Essex

British Library Cataloguing in Publication Data
Mason, S. (Stanley)
The small business finance raiser. – (Building
your business)
1. Small business – Great Britain – Finance
I. Title   II. Series
658.1′522   HG4027.7
ISBN 0 09 160750 7 (cased)
    0 09 160751 5 (paper)

Building Your Business

Series Editor: Tom Cannon

The last decade has witnessed a growing awareness of the importance of a healthy small business sector. The individuality, flexibility and creativity of the entrepreneur are recognized as vital to economic prosperity. Yet the same period has thrown up more and more challenges to the small firm. Competition has become more rigorous, while the need for efficiency and the effective application of resources has increased sharply. Perhaps the most valuable of these resources today is knowledge.

This series of books has been designed specifically for the entrepreneur, to bring to the owner and manager of the small firm vital areas of knowledge and information. The aim throughout has been to break down the barriers between theory and practice. The books are 'action-oriented' and this action-orientation is built into the texts themselves. Each book is broken down into self-contained Units. Each Unit sets out **Key Issues**, develops the issues and ends up with **Action Guidelines**. Wherever possible, examples are drawn from the actual experience of small business people. Each author is an expert in his own field but equally at home with the application of his expertise to the small firm.

Growing recognition of the needs of the small firm has led to a range of initiatives to provide assistance. Government at a national and local level, large companies, banks and voluntary agencies are actively seeking ways to help the owner and manager of the small business to thrive. However the key characteristic of this type of company is its dependence on individual effort and skill. The onus for survival and prosperity lies on the man or woman who turns these ideas into action.

This series focuses on the key areas of customers, money, people, the law, export and computers. The ideas presented will help provide the management expertise which leads to success.

Contents

Preface

Although this book is part of a series aimed at small businesses poised for growth, it is, in fact, equally relevant to new or established businesses of all sizes in all manufacturing or service ventures. It will also be of great value to executives and staff employed in all kinds of companies, providing for them the armoury they need to assist the business and to help them on their way up the ladder to success. The reason why the information set out is so vital revolves around one very important activity – raising finance – and the key to success is the business plan. It does not really matter whether you run a retail shop on the corner, or whether you are the Chief Executive of ICI – finance is the common thread. In a large company there are departments employed to handle all the planning, budgeting, forecasting and monitoring which are designed to pave the way to satisfactory lending propositions. If you are starting up, or operate a very small business, likely as not you will have to do all the planning yourself. But how do you plan your business with a view to raising finance? Not only is it hard work, but without experience it can become extremely complicated. Nevertheless, by using the information in this book, you can progress step by step and improve the chances of your success phenomenally.

For most small businesses, the bank manager is the lifeline. Without the overdraft it would all evaporate. Businessmen and women will be asked to pledge their houses, their life assurance, and anything else of value in their efforts to raise money to achieve their ideals. They are probably totally unaware of free advisory centres, government aid, grants, cheap loans, and a multitude of other facilities and benefits which may be available. Whatever is on offer, however, it cannot be won unless you are able to present an adequate case for finance. Lenders are very experienced professional people. They have seen thousands of applications cross their desks, and there is usually a queue of customers wishing to borrow money. Therefore, your presentation may fail unless you plan your business properly and prove to the lender that you can develop soundly and that you have good potential. Never presume that because you offer excellent security the lender will agree to grant you financial facilities. Such security cannot turn a bad application into a good one – but a good prospect may be ruined by a bad presentation. Hence, you need to develop a sound business plan in order to raise finance. But before you read on, remember one very important thing: lenders do not normally return presentations for amendment or revision; they either accept them in principle or reject them. As a result, you have only 'one shot' to make your mark. So read this book, and then make it your very best effort!

S. Mason

I
How Much Money Have You Got?

- What do you need to know about your business?
- Have you asked the right questions about your product/ service?
- What do you know about your competitors?
- Where do you go for finance?
- What form should your business take?
- How can you benefit from the tax situation?
- Are you financing debtors – How much is it costing you?
- What do you do in a cash crisis?

The idea of starting a business is easy; from then on, the going gets much rougher. And it does not matter whether you are new to business or an expert with a great deal of experience, the secret of success follows the same pattern.

- If you are starting from scratch, what do you need to do to avoid making serious mistakes that could cost you your savings and even the house in which you live?
- If you are already in business, have you made fundamental errors which are causing you to suffer headaches and sleepless nights?
- Even if you are coping reasonably well, where do you go from here?

Identifying your business

Let us look at some of the basics of business to put you on the right road to success. It is not an easy task – but it is not that difficult either if you take the trouble to plan your campaign properly. Before you do anything else, you should attempt to answer the following questions:

1 **What business are you in?** You may think this a daft question but the answer could surprise you – many people try to do too many things, or they change direction in mid-stream and then become confused. For example, a ladies' woollen knitwear manufacturer kept stating that his line of business was clothing. This term was too wide to define his business, and he almost failed because of lost orders – people do not want clothing. They want particular kinds of clothing.

   A road haulier became involved in rail, sea and air freight, and lost control of his business because he ended up trying to spread his few resources over every area of transport in which he operated.

   In both cases the businessmen did not identify the business they were in, which caused them to go astray.

2 **What specific product/service do you offer?** It should be described in detail. For example, you should not claim to be a knitwear manufacturer, but a ladies' woollen knitwear manufacturer – size range 10 to 16, in five basic designs, sporting three different colours. Now you can see your product in its real light and know exactly what you are making. As such, you can review it and make simple changes, for example, fewer desins, more (or fewer) colours, etc.

3 **Who are your customers?** Following the example above – ladies' woollen knitwear – your customers will be ladies aged between 18 and 30 in the UK (if you do not export), sold to retail shops, or by salesmen, or by direct mail. If you sell through other channels, you must consider the likes and dislikes of buyers and wholesalers whom you want to buy your product for their customers. Hence, although you are selling to ladies aged between 18 and 30, you may have to satisfy buyers who are completely different in sex, age, size and shape.

4 **Why do people buy products or services like yours?** Do they need your products for general use, for health reasons, in conjunction with other articles, because they are amusing, fashionable, or essential, or what? You cannot always assume that your products will be used exactly for the purpose you made them.

5 **Why will people buy your product/service?** Is it unique, cheaper, better quality, or what? If you cannot think of anything, you may be well advised to think about a new product or service that will attract customers.

6 **Can you identify specific customers and their reaction?** Do you have any firm orders, or promises of orders? Have customers written or told you what they think of your product/service?

After this, there are questions on the market and sales, which are very important features for you to consider.

1 **What do you know about your competitors?** Are their products/services of higher quality, better value for money, or more profitable?

2 **What are the major strengths and weaknesses of competitors?** Can you find a market gap for your product/service?

3 **Do you expect to compete on price?** If so, how do you expect to make a realistic profit? How have you arrived at your pricing? Are you falling into the trap of undercutting everyone else – in which case will you be slashing your own margins and running high risks? Have you worked out your breakeven position?

4 **How will you sell your product/service?** Through retailers, wholesalers, your own salesmen, agents, direct to the public, or how else?

5 **How will you distribute your product/service?** By yourself, with a team, through a distributor? And over which regional areas?

6 **How long can you survive before the first sales come through?** Have you enough finance to keep you going through the initial period?

Let us move on to your product/service itself and review some of the immediate problems that you might have to face.

1 **Is it ready for sale now?** If not, how far has it been developed, and how long will it take to get it to the marketplace? What will it cost you to produce – or what will be the cost of the equipment needed to offer the service?

2 **What are the snags between your present position and sales?** You should list these in detail to make sure that you understand the problems well.

3 **How can they be overcome?** How long will it take, and how much will it cost? Make sure that you can find adequate solutions within your financial means. Do not hang on to a business dream if you cannot find a way to make it work!

4 **How long will your product/service be marketable?** Will it be short-lived? Can it be developed into a range? Is this the 'first' product/service? Can you diversify into others?

5 **If you operate on an agency, licensee or franchisee basis, are you sure of the territory, duration, exclusivity, initial payment, royalties, etc?** What success has the product/service experienced in the past?

Next we come to an analysis of staff, finance and risks, which should be examined very carefully.

1 **What are the main skills you need to run your business?** Do the skills demanded and those acquired relate to each other? If not, can you gain access to them?

2 **What kinds of skilled/unskilled workers do you need?** How can you find them and attract them? Are there people available locally?

3 **How much money will you need before you can start?** Where will you get it? How much more will you need before cash starts flowing into the business?

4 **Where can you go to get finance and what do you have to do to get it?** How can you present your case? Will it be better to go to your family, friends, a bank, a financial institution, the EEC or the government – or whom?

5 **What major risks do you face by going ahead with your business?** How sensitive is your survival with each risk? How can you minimize the risks?

16

6 How soon will it be until the business can support you? Can you survive until then? If so, how?

You will need to provide sincere answers to all these questions if you want to establish a successful business and survive. It is no use skipping through most of them with self-assurance, believing that you know what you are doing and telling yourself there is no point in becoming involved in such an exercise. Most business failures result from people thinking that way, mainly because they close their minds to the realities of business life and the personal risks they face right from the start. There is no substitute for care, caution and professional advice.

Where do you start?

Every business starts with a plain sheet of paper. Thereafter, it is soon filled with figures relating to the amount of money you will need. This is the moment when you find out the real worth of your assets – that is everything you own when converted to cash and after all your debts are paid. The amount available will give you some idea of how much you can put into your business venture personally and it will also give some indication of how much you may be able to borrow. Lenders will want you to put more money in than they do. But let us have a look at your own worth before you ask others to help you.

Table 1 shows how you would set about assessing your own worth. On the face of it, you can lay your hands on £55,000, but this is an overestimation as you will see. It is not the amount you can actually raise for your business. Some items listed will be more saleable than others. You have to decide firstly if your car is needed, and whether your family should be put at risk by borrowing against your house almost up to its full equity value? In any case, neither the building society nor any other lender would lend you finance anywhere near £50,000; they would always look for a fair margin in case it had to be sold quickly. So how much would you expect to accumulate? Let us have another look and work out the true figure. (See Table 2.)

Internal sources of finance

Table 1

	£
Market value of your house	50,000
Other property	5,000
Car	5,000
Caravan	1,500
Life assurance policies	10,000
Shares/Government stock/Unit Trusts	3,000
Paintings/objets d'art	1,000
Coin/stamp collection	1,000
Building Society deposits	2,000
National Savings Certificates	500
Deposit account at the bank	500
Other	500
Assets	80,000

Less:	£	
Outstanding mortgage	18,000	
Personal loan – caravan	2,000	
Hire purchase – car	3,000	
Overdraft at bank	1,500	
Credit card payments	200	
Other bills outstanding	300	
Liabilities		25,000
Net value		55,000

Table 2

		£
House: £50,000 − £18,000 (mortgage) = £32,000	say	25,000
Other property	say	4,500
Car (you will want to keep the car)	—	—
Caravan: £5,000 − £2,000 (personal loan)	say	2,500
Life assurance policy: £10,000, surrender value	say	5,000
Shares	say	3,000
Paintings/collections	say	1,500
Building Society/National Savings Certificates	say	2,500
Deposit account/other	say	1,000
		45,000
Less:	£	
Hire purchase: car	3,000	
Overdraft at bank	1,500	
Credit card and bills	500	5,000
Total available		40,000

As you can see, the total available has dropped £15,000 from your original figure. Note also that if you use all of this amount, there will be nothing left in reserve.

External sources of finance

If you do not wish to use all your own money – or you need more to start with – you will have to look for other sources of finance. They may include the following:

Relatives Money from your wife, husband, parents, parents-in-laws, aunts, uncles (especially those that favour you), godparents, cousins (perhaps who are in business themselves), and any other relatives however remote may be the link. Borrow from relatives only if they do not need the money and can afford to lose it all. It may be possible that you can obtain tax relief on the loan if you qualify for the Business Expansion Scheme.

Friends You may have personal friends with resources who will lend you money. But do not forget to list associates who might help. Do not borrow from friends unless you value them. If they are interested in what you are trying to do, their advice will be good. If they are not interested, they will expect to do well out of you.

A bank   The banks are willing to help small businesses, but they judge every application on its merit. It will help if you already have an account with a bank because the manager will have some idea of your banking relationship and does not need to start from scratch (for example, getting references on you). Managers vary enormously; try to find one who is sympathetic to your needs – a change of manager is often more important to your business than a change of bank. And, most important, if you want finance from a bank, go to the bank manager before you need to borrow.

The main banks can offer all the services you will need, and, no doubt, you will return showered with literature on many useful schemes. But you will be expected to go to your local bank manager rather than to the head office of the bank, or its departments.

The bank may ask for a charge on your house, and, if it is mortgaged to a building society, for a second mortgage charge. If things go wrong and it has to be sold, the building society is paid first, the bank is next and you get the rest. There will be very little left at the end of the day. So think carefully before you allow the bank to take a charge on your house, because there is your family to think of – they live there too! It is not a formality and there could be serious repercussions. A bank will foreclose on your property if you fail to repay money owed to them and it has been given as security. Therefore, do try to offer other types of security if possible.

Government and EEC aid   There are many schemes to help you on your way – even to start up (for example, the Loan Guarantee Scheme) – as well as special cheap loans from the EEC. Many of them are operated by the banks on behalf of the government or the EEC, so make sure that your bank manager tells you about them. In addition, a number of free advice agencies exist, as well as numerous grants which may be applicable to you. Do not forget the Development Agencies in Wales, Scotland and Northern Ireland.

Merchant banks   Although merchant banks are likely to deal with medium/larger businesses, they can bring investors and businesses together where the product or service is attractive.

International banks   These are beginning to attract businesses in Britain. You should not feel sensitive about doing business with, say,

20

a US or a Swedish bank if their services seem more attractive.

Private investors These include solicitors, accountants, stock-brokers and insurance brokers – all of whom may know of individuals who could be potential investors.

Venture capital companies These offer to take a stake in your business and provide the 'seed' capital to start it growing. You may get funds but you lose part of your company in the early stages at least.

It is worth approaching every avenue to find the finance you need. Do not be too concerned when asking for money. You are not stealing it – just borrowing it to get you started.

What form of business?

Generally, businesses take one of three forms:

1   As a **sole trader** you are the proprietor of the business but, legally, your business assets are the same as your personal assets. If you become bankrupt both will be sold to repay creditors. If the business assets are not enough to pay the debts, you will be made to sell your house, your furniture and everything you own to satisfy others. Therefore, if things go wrong, you and your family will suffer very much.

2   **A partnership** is legally the same as a sole trader, except that there are two or more people acting as proprietors instead of one. The rules of bankruptcy are the same – all the personal assets of the partners can be realized to pay the debts of the business. If you go into partnership you will certainly need a partnership agreement, drawn up by a solicitor, clearly stating the proportions in which you provide capital and share profits. There may be other provisions laying down interest rates on loans to the partnership and restricting the rights of an ex-partner to have a similar business within, say, twenty miles. It is very important to choose a suitable partner. If there are personality clashes or regular disagreements you will spend more time fighting each other than furthering the progress of the business.

3   **A limited company** is a legal 'person' in its own right. It can

make contracts, own property, sue and be sued, and be made to pay fines for criminal offences. With a limited company you will not be self-employed; you will be employed as a director of the company. A company can have a sole director but it is better to have two – with your husband or wife, if no-one else. In the event of the insolvency of the company, your liability will be limited to the share capital which you have subscribed, say £100. Companies do not become bankrupt, they go into liquidation or are compulsorily wound-up. Lenders seek security from sole traders and partnerships for loans offered. They may well do so from limited companies, but because your liability is limited only to the share capital, say, £100, personal guarantees by the directors are often sought against any loans. If not, they may insist that you put in a lot of your own money as share capital. Nevertheless, there are a lot of advantages in operating a limited company. For example:

- Share capital can easily be transferred to others – although private company shares are not easily marketable.
- The company structure provides a proper regulated form for the business (with its own rules, directors, secretary, etc.).
- More capital can be raised in many forms.
- The company is a legal entity on its own, unaffected by death or resignation of directors.
- A company has a more permanent, reliable form in the eyes of customers and suppliers.
- The company may be floated evenutally on the stock market.

On the other hand, a limited company has certain responsibilities which do not affect sole traders or partnerships:

- A limited company has less privacy – accounts and returns have to be filed with the Registrar of Companies.
- Accounts have to be audited, generally to a higher standard than that required for a sole trader.
- There are big differences in taxation between the limited company and the sole trader or partnership.

There may be many reasons why you may choose one form of operation for your business in preference to another. You are advised to ask your accountant and solicitor for their views. However, one of the main factors may be taxation. Sole traders and partners pay income tax; limited companies pay corporation tax. A summary of tax considerations is set out in Table 3.

Table 3 *Tax considerations for limited company versus sole trader*

	Limited company	Sole trader
Tax basis	30 per cent of profit	Income tax on profit after allowances
Retained profit	Taxed at corporation tax rate	Taxed at income tax higher rates
Timing of payment	Directors' salaries immediately under PAYE	Twelve to twenty-three months later (depending on accounting year)
Losses	Can normally be set off only against company profits	Can be set off against other income
Losses conversion	Can be used in a company reconstruction	Can still be used if the business is converted to a partnership or a company
Retrospective loss allowance for new business	Not given	Allowance for four years against general income of previous three years
National insurance	Substantially higher total contribution for directors as employees (but some additional benefits)	Lower total contribution as self-employed

	Limited company	Sole trader
Use of car	Can belong to company with favourable treatment of private use	Private use taxed as a proportion agreed with Inspector of Taxes
Pension provision	Possibility of company pension scheme giving more tax relief	Self-employed retirement annuity only

If you decide to apply for venture capital you will need to be a limited company, because the lender will want to take part of your equity (shares in your company).

Working from home

Some people dive into business as though they must start at the top. They decide to buy or lease premises, buy vans, machinery, etc., and use up much of the money they have. In reality, it may be good common sense to start from home; sometimes it is practical to begin by making products in a shed, or using your home from which to offer a service. The main value of using your home is that it is cheap. Fitting out an office or a workshop will cost money; then there is the expense of rent, rates, insurance, and so on. If you begin at home, you will have time to get organized and build up sales to the point where the business can operate properly. However, at home there are many distractions; there is a tendency to be a little undisciplined – for example, letting odd periods slip by, or starting work late, in spite of the fact that you save time by not having to travel – but, if you are married, your husband or wife may be able to help you, thus cutting down costs. Whether you need the prestige of an office address, at first, depends on the nature of your business. Sometimes it is possible to find another small business with space to spare, which is prepared to offer a room, or maybe just a desk, possibly with someone there who might take messages for you.

Before you move ahead

You may have fantastic ability in producing your product/service, and your selling ability could be equally fantastic. You might be able to sell fridges to Eskimos and sand to the Arabs, but that does not make you a good businessman or ensure that your business will be successful. There are many fine points – even beyond the planning function which you will come to shortly – that you ought to understand. One of the most important is to recognize that there is a wide difference between profit and cash. Profit is the engine; cash is the fuel. As your sales increase you must not automatically assume that the increase in profit will show itself as cash in your bank account. So many business people rub their hands with glee at the profits they are making and then try to puzzle out why they are going bust. The reason is that during growth they have run out of money – it is all tied up in stocks, work-in-progress and with debtors. For all these items you will pay interest on the money you borrowed.

Let us take debtors as a particular feature. Until a customer settles an account with you, your business will be financing him. If payment of £1000 is delayed for three months, and the interest rate to you is 14 per cent on your overdraft, the cost of supporting your customer on that bill alone will be £35. Multiply this sum by thirty such customers and the cost of interest will be £1050. There is also the problem of bad debts, when customers fail to pay at all, which means that you must apply firm credit control procedures or it will cost you dearly. You should not be too hasty to accept customers before you know their quality and creditworthiness. You can obtain that information through bankers' references or credit-rating agencies. When this is done and you are satisfied, all your customers should be clearly aware of your credit terms before trading begins. If you are in too great a hurry to start business and fail to take these precautions you may find the result becomes very expensive in time, money and frustration.

When assessing the finance you need, you should include this element of debtor interest which is often missed out. At the end of each month you should check the average number of days your customers are taking to pay. This can be worked out as follows:

$$\frac{\text{debts} \times 365 \text{ days}}{\text{annual sales}} = \text{number of days credit}$$

Therefore if you have debtors owing £20,000 and annual sales of £100,000, the equation is:

$$\frac{£20,000 \times 365}{£100,000} = 73 \text{ days credit}$$

If the average payment in your particular industry is 45 days then you are giving customers an extra 28 days extra credit at your own expense. Hence, however good a technician or a salesman you are, it is vital that you become aware of this and other important features of business.

Overtrading

The problems of overtrading are not often recognized and, in fact, you will rarely find much detail about the subject in business books. Yet it is one of the most fundamental errors that one can make, which will almost certainly lead to bankruptcy or liquidation if not corrected. The strangest thing about overtrading is the fact that the business appears to be expanding faster than ever, and trade seems to be improving all the time, even though the business may be in danger of collapse within a short time. How is that possible? How, if the business is expanding, orders are coming in fast and furious, and the turnover is rising all the time, can one consider that peril is at hand? But it is possible. There are a number of features which relate to overtrading and you should take heed of them to avoid such dangers.

- In most businesses there is a tendency to expand and progress. The aim will be to increase sales and profitability within the confines of the production or service functions. This is an admirable quality and the natural function of business development. In normal circumstances, all works fairly well in an atmosphere of strict competition. But if there is too much emphasis on sales, a business might suffer the effects of 'turnover syndrome', which means that it concentrates too much on increasing the sales figure at all costs. This is a very dangerous policy to pursue, because the more you sell, the more finance you will require to expand. A high turnover does not necessarily mean that you are making excellent profits. You need to work out a relationship between your sales, profits, finance, production and manpower.

For example, if a business employs ten staff for sales of £50,000 and the profit is £5000, how much profit will it make on sales of £100,000? Easy! £10,000! Wrong! It would probably be necessary to employ more staff, increase the borrowing arrangements with the bank for the extra materials required (perhaps at high interest rates), spend more on premises and equipment relating to the expansion (remember you are wearing out machinery if you use it more, and it will need to be replaced), and so on. The end result is that you do not make profits of £10,000. In fact, you will probably make less profit than £5000 because of the rambling development of the business.

The problem is clearly that the business is trying to do too much, and it stands out a mile that sales volume and massive turnover do not necessarily mean that your business is being successful.

● What is the main effect of overtrading? The answer is a cash crisis. You must not believe, however, that every time you have a cash crisis it is the result of overtrading. There may be other reasons. Nevertheless, it is the most common cause of the complaint. Margins are often too low. You may feel that you have to reduce them to such low levels because competition is severe and if you failed to cut them your customers would look elsewhere for their supplies or services. That may well be the case, but how far do you want to walk the plank until you fall into the water? Cutting margins is the easiest way to compete in business. Anyone can offer goods at less than cost and find customers. If you cut margins too much, you will more than likely gain custom, but the result will be that the turnover syndrome will operate and eventually you will have a cash crisis.

● Many inexperienced business people cannot understand why a high turnover does not mean that more profits are being made. After all, the policy at Tesco, the supermarket chain, was

'Pile it high, sell it cheap'. If such a policy is good enough for a public company, why cannot it be copied elsewhere? There is no doubt that it can, but certain operations need to be carefully controlled. These relate to influx of customers, a 'mix' of goods (in that while some may be 'loss-leader' items, others will provide good margins), tight control of finance, containment of staff during expansion, limitation of distribution and production costs, utilization of every part of the premises, good marketing and promotion methods, etc., etc.

- The only way to resolve the problem of overtrading is by use of a sound business plan. You must be clear in your mind that it will never be entirely eliminated mainly because both expansion and competition exist. It is not sensible to withhold development of sales in order to ensure that there is always cash available. Equally, it would be nonsense to maintain exceedingly high margins where competitors are offering the same product or service at a much lower cost. You will need to examine your business, its capability and potential, and operate a cash flow very carefully to ensure that you survive and remain profitable. These features are outlined later in this book.

Cash crises

Inevitably, cash crises occur fairly regularly in business. You will need to keep a cool head when they occur. Whatever the reasons for any particular crisis, you should take the following steps swiftly:

1 Keep cool – do not panic.
2 Draw up a list of expected 'cash in' and 'cash out'.
3 Indicate clearly which payments have priority.
4 Advise your bank manager/financial institution of the problem and ask for advice – perhaps a rearrangement/increase of funding.
5 Do not avoid creditors. Answer their telephone calls and letters. Try to pay them 'something'.
6 If you keep your word, creditors will learn to trust you. Ask your accountant to approach them for you.

7 Recheck your production/service operations and find ways to reduce expenditure.

8 Try to sell stock which is not moving; offer cash discounts to larger debtors; and dispose of spare plant or property, where possible.

Once you have stabilized the situation, you should focus your attention on your business plan. The units ahead will guide you accordingly.

Action Guidelines

1   Calculate your real worth!

_____

_____

2   Who can you borrow from?

_____

_____

3   How much could you raise to finance your business?

_____

_____

4   If you needed more later on, where will it come from?

_____

_____

5   What kind of business are you in?

_____

_____

6   Who are your customers?

_____

_____

7   What benefits are they looking for?

_____

_____

8   Why should they buy your product/service?

_____

_____

9   List the points which make your product/service stand out from those
    of competitors!

    _____

    _____

10 List the risks if your plans fail – to both you and your family!

    _____

    _____

11 Consider the worst that could happen. Can you afford it?

    _____

    _____

12 Work out the implications of rapid growth. What difference will it make
    to your working life? What changes will occur in your personal life?
    Is it worth it ?

    _____

    _____

    _____

13 Make a detailed assessment of your financial needs over the period
    for which you are raising finance. Be clear how much you need and
    what you need it for – and allow a margin for error!

    _____

    _____

14 Work out how you will repay loans! Do not attempt anything if lack of
    success will make it impossible to at least pay off loan interest.

    _____

    _____

    _____

    _____

2
How to Prepare a Business Plan that Works

- What will you do if you do not have a plan?
- How do you start planning?
- Can you assess your business and its potential?
- How does marketing fit into the plan?
- Do you know how to set the right price?
- How to set up the right selling techniques?
- Who are your customers and how do you reach them?

Why a plan is necessary

What will you do if you do not have a plan? You can sell your product to customers – if you can find them; you can set a price for your goods or service that they will pay which might be too low to allow your business to survive; you can keep going to stay in business – but you will be working in the dark. So what are you supposed to do? After all, the business keeps you busy most of the time – there is nothing much left of you to do anything else! If that is the case, you are wasting time working at random – thrashing about like a person unable to swim who is thrown into a deep pool. The chances are that unless you can co-ordinate your actions you will sink. It is the same with your business, except that the co-ordination is called planning.

The importance of planning cannot be overstated, because without it your business can have no direction. If you fail to set plans properly, you will be at the mercy of competitors, customers, bankers and financiers, and you will soon lose sight of your main objectives and then flounder. It is almost impossible to survive if you carry on your business solely on a day-to-day basis. Planning is the means by which you can make the most efficient use of your resources – cash, credit, machinery, sales, manpower, etc. It is the only way that you can keep on course. Do not be misled into thinking that only long-term planning is useful, because short-term planning covers many uncertainties which you have to face every day, every week, every month, every year.

Short-range plans usually run for a year or less. You will have to make them flexible as everyday problems and decisions may cause the situation to fluctuate widely against your original assessment. A rail or transport strike, for example, may bring your business to a halt, but if you have borrowed on overdraft the bank will not be too concerned about its own position because interest on the borrowed amount still continues to accrue daily – strike or no strike. Hence, you must be prepared for 'unfair' situations which affect your business. At other times, you may lose small or large contracts, or sudden cancellations might take place. In many cases, contingency plans may allow you to cope with serious problems, but in normal circumstances only a slight adjustment may be needed to keep you on the right course. At least, with your short-range plan, you will know the direction in which you are going with each touch of the rudder, instead of swerving violently from one chaotic position to another.

Long-range plans involve periods of longer than one year. Long-range planning is a means by which you can look to the future with positive aims in mind. You should identify the targets you want your business to reach, taking into account many factors which could affect the plan. These may include internal or external economic problems, government restrictions, an allowance for labour disputes, material shortages, international difficulties, financial constraints, decline in industry or recession, and so on. Despite some, or all, of these factors, it is very important for you to set goals for your business; these can be adjusted as conditions change.

What do you need to know before you start?

It is not possible to develop plans without looking into the future, and to do this you will need to rely very much on forecasting based on various kinds of information. Forecasting is an exercise which should be carried out regularly at monthly, quarterly, half-yearly and yearly intervals so that you can compare the results with those on which you based your original plan. But before you arrive at that stage, you ought to look at some of the principles of planning which are set out below.

- You must clearly identify the goals to be achieved by your plan. It must have a clear and definite purpose.

- The information in the plan must be thorough and meaningful. Forecasts will help but you should use other sources, such as past records, performance experience, etc. Make sure, however, that you do not get bogged down in a mass of irrelevant information.

- You should co-ordinate every element of the plan. Co-ordination of your activities is very important to the success of your business. For example, if you run out of money at the time orders roll in, you may find that you delay the start of production; if you fail to time your marketing effort correctly, you may find that you are overstocked with manufactured goods waiting for customers' orders, in which case you will lock up working capital and storage space; if you do not harmonize your production with the sales effort, it may lead to overstocking, underdelivery, and disappointed customers who will go to competitors and never come back.

- You will need to set standards and monitor performance so that you are always aware of the situation.

- Plans must be flexible to allow for adjustment. It is no use sticking rigidly, on principle, to the original plan if large-scale changes have occurred. The plan is your guideline, not an anchor.

- Everyone else employed in your business should be aware of your business plan so that they understand what is involved and work together to reach the same goals.

- Most important of all is that your plan should be *achievable*. It is discouraging and frustrating to set a very ambitious target which is impossible to reach. There are many people now working hard for others who once had their own business; their target was to 'become a millionaire before they reached the age of 40'. It was unachievable and they failed trying to do it.

There are three other features which ought to be considered in the light of long-range planning. Firstly, it has already been mentioned that your staff should be aware of your business plan. Without their co-operation all your efforts are likely to be inhibited. However, there is the important element of communication. We tend to explain complicated information to other people and believe that they understand it and view it in the same way as ourselves. This is not always the case. People often tend to listen to those features they want to hear and miss the important details. Hence, you should be very careful to make certain that you communicate effectively so that others know exactly what you intend.

Secondly, it is of vital importance for your plans to be consistent. Nothing is worse than having to heave the rudder widely to port or starboard because of a sudden emergency. The effect on the staff and the business in such cases may be catastrophic. Inevitably, there will be occasions when the main plan needs to be adjusted, but such movement should be limited. Therefore, you should take great care in preparing your plan and make sure it is consistent.

Thirdly, there is the value of numbers in the plan. In some cases, the businessman identifies a plan and keeps all the figurework in his head. This is often due to the fact that he wishes to keep the information secret from competitors and feels more safe this way. But everything should be enumerated in a plan, down to the last detail, for unless it is set out like that the business will proceed like a ship without a sail, and no one will be the wiser.

Your business cannot possibly function properly if you leave all matters to chance. You may be very lucky and succeed; more likely you will not. It is important that you follow the rules and bring into focus all your resources by means of planning, which will identify your aims and objectives and help to promote the controls that are part and parcel of your plans. In this way, you can promote sales, set financial targets, ensure a reasonable return on capital and investment, and guide your business successfully.

Before you embark on setting your objectives and goals, and preparing budgets and forecasts, you would be well advised to look at four features of strategic planning, which you should develop within your plan. Examine them well, for they hold the key to your future prospects.

1 *Strengths*
   (a) What are the most advantageous features of your business?
   (b) Are your products/services in demand?
   (c) Is your business image/customer goodwill at a high level?
   (d) Do you have a really good salesforce?
   (e) Is your staff highly efficient technically?
   (f) Do you have an edge on your competitors' products/services?
   (g) Have you established a good financial base?
   (h) Can you improve the strengths in your business?

2 *Weaknesses*
   (a) Are you weak in financial support?
   (b) Is your plant and machinery becoming obsolescent?
   (c) Are you coping adequately with competitors?
   (d) Is your product/service in decline?
   (e) Are you losing customer loyalty?
   (f) Do you have other products/services tested and ready for the market?
   (g) How can you remedy the weaknesses in your business?

3 *Opportunities*
   (a) Can you find new domestic markets?
   (b) Are you able to improve your financial position?
   (c) Would a takeover or merger help you?
   (d) Are there other products/services you could develop?
   (e) Should you go into the export market?
   (f) How can you improve on your current business performance?
   (g) Are you looking for opportunities? If so, are you looking widely enough?

4   *Threats*

  (a) Is your planning weak?
  (b) Are you affected by changing technology?
  (c) Will competitors take a larger share of the market?
  (d) Will foreign companies intrude into your market?
  (e) Are your staff careless and complacent?
  (f) Is the life-cycle of your product/service ready to decline?
  (g) How will economic/political uncertainties affect you over the next two years?
  (h) Is your financial situation threatened?
  (i) Will there be a recession?
  (j) Are you prepared for such problems, should they arise?

The list is not exhaustive and you are strongly urged to examine your business very carefully in the light of each of these features. It may well be that after analysis you will see your business in a different light, and set objectives at a different angle from that you had considered earlier.

Marketing

We next move on to marketing, which is another important feature to be considered. Forget the mystique! Do not allow other people who cannot grasp the use of marketing to put you off. It is vital to your success in business. Having said that, deep down you may think that marketing is complicated and expensive, and best left to bigger firms – wrong! Good marketing is essential to the survival of the smaller business, let alone its growth. Mistakes made and opportunities lost by larger companies are rarely recorded in their profit and loss accounts, but the smaller business has to be right most of the time. Never forget that the proper use of marketing is one way in which the odds can be shortened in your favour.

But what is marketing? Let us not go into the realms of different definitions conjured up by academics. We want to know about real life marketing. It is a means of effective selling and good management, not only of your resources, but also of those elements of your business by which you sell and make profits. The first step is to decide on the marketing 'mix' which is right for your business. The main activities which determine this 'mix' are:

1 Selling, distribution, delivery
2 Product/service development
3 Advertising
4 Pricing, discounts, commissions
5 After-sales service, spares

These activities will be visible to your customers, but there are other very important marketing activities, also part of the 'mix', which mostly go on behind the scenes. These are:

6 Market, customer, and product research
7 Planning

The marketing plan draws all these activities together, analyses your present position, states the objectives, and pinpoints plans for action. Of particular importance is the fact that you must care about your customers – their needs and problems – and translate that care into properly organized marketing activities. If you simply want to make profits, your customers will soon recognize this fact and probably drift away.

You will not be able to make many of the key decisions in marketing until all the facts have been collected. Once the research has been completed, you can draw up your plan of action. The purpose of market research is to reduce the area of uncertainty in making business decisions. This involves:

1 **Corporate planning** If you do not know where you are in business, you have no idea where you are going. You should have a rough idea of the market in which you operate, and whether it is growing or shrinking.

2 **Market planning** You not only need to think where you will be in five years' time, you want to know how you can increase sales and profits in the next twelve months. Information is necessary on the market prospects of the industries in which your customers are operating, and the prospects for those particular customers. Analysis of sales and customer data will also show up regional and industry gaps. With the rough size of market data split by regions, it is possible to work out a regional pattern for your business.

3 **Product service development** Market research will provide data on the likely effect on sales volume and profitability of

slimming down the range of goods offered. This is often a better and quicker way of improving both profits and service to the customer than additions to the range. New product or service development also needs help from the market researcher. First of all, you need to discover the approximate size of the market, and the level and nature of competition; then, you should refine the product or service specification; and finally it will be necessary to carry out test marketing operations.

4 **Measuring effectiveness** This includes research into the attitudes of your customers and distributors, your products, and competing products and companies. Useful information may be obtained from customers and non-customers on their reasons for buying one product instead of another. Price and volume indications can also be obtained from the marketplace by studying competing products/services, or analysing those which serve the same purpose.

Sources of information
The first hurdle is to look at your main sources of market research information:

1 **Internal records** Most businesses have a wealth of information on their own files waiting to be analysed and used. Order books, invoices, sales representatives' and service reports, inquiry and return guarantee forms, etc., are all useful sources.

2 **Published information** There is a tremendous amount of information available from government departments, trade associations, the technical press, the banks, local reference libraries, chambers of commerce and so on. Advice is also obtainable from the Small Firms Information Centres of the Department of Industry.

3 **Field research** This can be carried out on a wide variety of levels. You may carry out this type of exercise asking specific questions to which you need to know answers. The most usual target groups are your customers and competitors' customers, but others may be your suppliers and distributors.

Do not fall into the trap of going overboard on research and ending up with so much information that you are confused. Set down on paper those things you need to know and limit yourself to that list. But beware that you do not miss out any main features or you will have to research them quickly in order to fit them into your main plan!

Pricing

You hardly need to be told that pricing plays a critical role in marketing, and that it cannot be isolated from the other factors, such as product/service design, sales/service arrangements, and promotion – which influence demand. What is the right price to charge for a product? The answer generally is 'What the market will bear'. Does that mean the price at which you can sell the largest amount of your product/service, or perhaps the highest price at which you will sell at all? In reality, the right price is the one which will bring the largest contribution to overheads and profit. In markets where the price is sensitive, the higher you set your price the fewer units you will sell – but the contribution of each unit will be high with regard to profit and overheads. For example, if you sell 100 units at £2.00 each, and they cost you £1.50 each, your profit will be £50; if you charge £2.50 each, you will sell, say, only 50 units, but your profit will be the same. The advantage is that you can use less employees, machinery, finance, office work, etc., by the second method.

Beware of chasing turnover at all costs. Many businesses, small and large, fail with order books bulging with unprofitable work. If pricing is to be worked out correctly, you must know how much your products cost to make or how much your services actually cost you. This should be defined as the direct cost of labour and material, plus those costs which are directly related to the product/service. Do not forget to include every single item of expenditure. These amounts have to be added together and then divided by the number of units or service calls to work out how much your unit/call costs you. Then you add on your profit margin. Getting the price right for an existing product is relatively easy; all you need is the nerve and the determination to go on increasing your price until it is quite clear that you have gone too far, and your sales are falling substantially. At that point, hold your price and try to cut your costs back to restore your profitability, rather than cut the price too quickly. If you cannot improve your margins when selling fewer units or carrying out fewer service calls, then you will have to reduce the price. There are, of course, problems in setting high targets, but it is the correct, fundamental strategy. A much more difficult problem is setting the right price for a new product, or quoting the right price for a service to be provided to a customer you do not know. The advice offered to you is as follows:

1   Make up your mind about the lowest price that you will consider. Whatever you want to achieve – even if it is buying your way into a market – there is a minimum price below which it is simply not worth it.

2   Ask your customers and potential customers or use market researchers.

3   Try to find out as much as you can about your competitors' prices but do not be mesmerized by them. It is not necessary to undercut everybody in sight to break into a market. Try to position your product/service; weigh it up as best as you can – its good points and its bad points – then try to decide whereabouts in the price range it should fit.

4   Try to guess what benefit your customers are going to get from using your product.

5   Do not be too afraid of overpricing; it is easier to come down than to go up, and very few companies go out of business through overpricing; underpricing can and does lead to disaster time and time again.

Selling

Selling is a special field all on its own. If you do not sell then you are not in business. How have you tackled this problem, and by what means do you sell? The first idea is usually to employ salespeople. It is far better to employ them on a 'commission only' basis – they earn only when they sell – but the world is not always ideal and most will ask for a basic wage, plus commission.

Most salespeople are order-takers and trouble-shooters, spending a comparatively small proportion of their time on positive selling. Nevertheless, they are the vital (and often the only) link between the business and the customer. How do they spend their time?

Travelling, waiting in the outer office, or sitting face to face with the customer? How can they be helped to reduce unproductive time? Perhaps by rearrangement of regional responsibility, by greater use of the telephone, for example, using tele-sales people, or by direct mail shots? Are salespeople told of your business sales message – the good points of the business and the product/service, and how they compare with competitors? Do they know the broad outline of the marketing plan and what part, in terms of turnover, profits, and new and old business, they each have to play? Do they make their contribution to the build-up of the sales budget, and are they listened to when they complain, as they always do, about the factory and the sales administration office? Is their salary related in some way to their performance?

If the business is to expand, it is important to ensure that the volume of sales increases. There are two main methods of increasing sales volume:

1 Marketing penetration
2 Market expansion

By the first method you will seek to increase the usage rate of your products by current customers, or attract non-customers to buy them. You may also achieve market growth by developing new uses for your products, or by increasing your market share and challenging the market positions held by competitors. The second method involves entering new market segments, for example, by going into new geographical areas, by exporting, etc., or by a policy of planned innovation, that is developing new products/services. The following activities can be listed as alternative strategies:

1 Improving the sales of present products/services in existing markets (penetration).
2 Finding new markets for present products/services (penetration).
3 Marketing new products/services in existing markets (expansion).
4 Marketing new products/services in new markets (expansion).

You should examine your product/service ranges and evaluate their potential for growth. It may be beneficial to improve the design of a product or offer a better after-sales service. On the other hand, the time may have come for some sharp pruning of the range. Sales might be improved by selling through wholesalers whose contacts in the retail trade are much more extensive. Deliveries direct to shops would help to ensure that goods are available for the public to buy.

Sales of existing products might also be improved by adding other pack sizes, or different colourings/flavourings, or even more attractive packaging. Sales of existing products may be increased by opening up business with non-traditional outlets. For example, selling toys or children's clothing in grocery supermarkets – and so the opportunities come to mind. Whatever you decide, you must ask yourself:

- Does your proposed product/service meet a need which your market research has identified?
- Is the demand for your proposed product/service likely to increase?
- If so, by how much, and over what period of time?
- If not, what steps will you take to develop new ones which will become profitable?

If you can find answers to these questions you may be well on the way to success. There are too many warehouses which look like museums – full of stock – because the firm failed to assess the situation properly in the first place.

Your market should be divided into 'territories'. Thereafter, projected market figures for salespeople would be divided into those territories. The progress of sales could then be checked easily and any corrective action could be taken in time. Sales territories should be designed so that they are relatively compact and have clearly defined boundaries. The costs of selling may be compared over territories and market sectors, and sales statistics should be gathered and analysed relating to:

1 Orders received
2 Sales invoiced
3 Orders outstanding for earliest possible delivery

4 Orders outstanding for delivery at specific future times

Sales statistics could also show comparative data over a period of two or more years, and by product group or service if necessary. When this information is gathered you will have a complete picture of your selling pattern and its prospects.

Product planning

All products have a life limitation which varies enormously. The Volkswagen (Beetle) car lasted forty years; the skateboard craze about nine months. In the fashion business, the product life-cycle can be as short as twelve months. Industrial products and service industries tend to be long-lived, but they too change, both in design and performance, and eventually many disappear. At any given time, therefore, a product or service is at a certain point in its life-cycle. Plotted on a graph, a typical product life-cycle will take the shape shown in Figure 1.

Figure 1 *A typical product life-cycle*

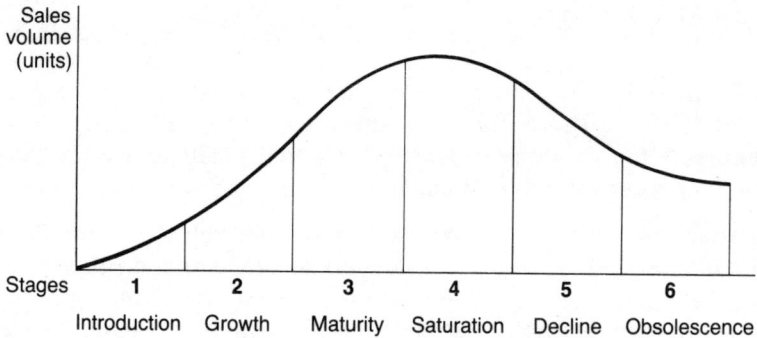

There comes a time when product redesign and marketing extensions can no longer arrest decline. Therefore, well before this point, you should have developed new products to replace the old, or moved into a new service operation.

Product/service planning is very important because your success will largely depend on the development of new products/services, the elimination of obsolescent or unprofitable products/services, the improvement of current products/services, and a full sales-service for the range of products/services. You should carefully consider the following points:

1 What markets are to be supplied?
2 What kind of product is needed?
3 What benefits should the product provide?
4 What is the level of demand for specific products?
5 What is the nature of competition in specific markets?

Too frequently markets are entered by businesses which do not answer these fundamental questions. In particular, they fail to assess the nature of competition and the likely reactions of competitors.

Publicity

Advertising, sales promotion and public relations are some of the methods by which you might be able to achieve profitable sales. The message must be tailored to the market you want to attack. And do not forget that markets are made up of people buying for themselves or for their companies. The information you need to acquire is:

- Who are they?
- Where are they?
- How many of them are there?
- Why do they want the product?
- What are they going to use it for?

The most usual ways of getting your message across are by:

Press advertising
Brochures and technical manuals
Mail shots
Exhibitions
Public relations

There is no answer to the question 'How much should we spend on publicity?' The required level of expenditure will be determined by the nature of your business, the level of competition, and the communication effectiveness of the other elements in the marketing 'mix'.

Whether you manufacture products or offer services you will need the support of well-designed schemes of promotion. This does not mean that you are fated to incur heavy advertising costs. Effective promotions can be designed within reasonably limited budgets. On the other hand, you should not expect too much from advertising; it is only part of the total marketing effort and by itself it is not sufficient for success. Product quality and availability should not be neglected; spending money on promoting goods is useless if the goods are not in the shops when the advertising message goes out. Large companies as well as small ones sometimes fail to ensure that their products are available for the public to see and buy before their advertising campaigns start. Before you start designing a publicity campaign, you should ask yourself the following questions:

- Have you set aside any part of your budget for promotion?
- Have you managed to get free press editorials from the local/ national press?
- Have you considered specialist trade exhibitions organized by the Department of Industry/British Overseas Trade Board?
- Are you sure your products are available and can meet the demand you intend to generate?

What do you put in your business plan?

So far, in the planning process, we have analysed a number of different areas. Now is the time to draw them all together to allow you a means by which you can operate your plans. This is done by devising a business plan which contains many things you need to recognize about your business, plus an action plan. The most usual headings covered are as follows:

1   Present situation of your business

2 Problems and opportunities

3 Objectives

4 Budget

5 Action

    (a) Product service development, sales, publicity, etc.

    (b) Who is responsible for which operations?

    (c) Timing elements for each product/service

6 Resources and organization

An analysis of the present position of your business leads to a statement of its main problems and opportunities. The objectives state what the business intends to achieve, expressed in specific terms. The budget translates these objectives into a profit and loss account for the company, to which the marketing plan will make its contribution. The action part of the plan is the most important part of all. Anyone can plan to increase market share by 25 per cent, but working out how to achieve it in the real world is difficult; and succeeding in practice is a very tough job. The action part of the plan should not only be specific in terms of what has to be done, but also in terms of who has to do it, and when. It should be split into a series of plans relating to the various activities shown above. The resources and organization have to be worked out at the same time as the financial budget is prepared, otherwise there will be no money available when the times comes to employ more salespeople, or design a new brochure, or redesign the product. It is very important that the plan is revised during the course of the year to accommodate changes.

Therefore your first business planning task is to find out all the facts, but the process should not be held up until they are all available. Objectives can often be set with very little research undertaken, and improved selling effort is a matter of common sense and organization. Of one thing you may be certain: if you can provide your own finance, or get it from family or friends, your plan may be devised and used without comment or criticism. However, if you go to a bank or a financial institution, they will expect you to present them with a plan that is professional and achievable. There is no doubt that you can do it yourself, but make sure that you take time and trouble to get it right. If it becomes slipshod because you did not follow the plan above, it will soon show. After all, professional lenders are reviewing businesses every day of the year. What do you put in/leave out? Easy! Follow the planning schematic in this unit carefully. Put in no more than the necessary items, and leave out the rest. You want to provide a plan for your business which can be read fairly swiftly by others – they do not wish to be presented with the sequel to *War and Peace*!

In this unit we have discussed how you can put together a plan to guide your business on a true course. Most of the tasks you have to carry out will seem strange because you probably have not done them before. But there will be sound benefits to your business if you build up your future plans using a jigsaw method with each part fitting in neatly against the next. If you simply shrug and ignore the advice it will almost certainly result in difficulty, if not disaster. Even with it you depend very much on your product/ service and its acceptability to customers. Nevertheless, it is far more sensible to be forewarned and forearmed with a proper plan than to dive into markets on a wing and a prayer. If you start with your strengths, weaknesses, opportunities and threats, you will soon find out.

Checklist

1   Identify your objectives. Write down the end results you wish to achieve and state them clearly, briefly and accurately.

2   Plan your activities. Decide on the major activities which must be performed – immediately, short-term and long-term.

3   Organize your programme with a list of things to be done, arranged in order of priority. Ask yourself:
     What is its purpose?
     Why is it necessary?
     Where should it be done?
     When should it be done?
     And how?

4   Prepare a work schedule. Set a time limit for each step in your programme. Do not allow time to pass without definite action taking place.

5   Establish review procedures. Determine where and when you will make reviews and necessary adjustments. Update long-term plans regularly.

6 Maintain channels of communication. Keep everyone in your business fully informed.

7 Develop co-operation. Improve motivation, reduce misunderstanding and friction.

8 Set responsibilities and accountability for all staff. You will get the best out of them if their work is meaningful.

9 Examine your strengths and weaknesses.

10 Do not overtrade. Avoid making targets dependent solely on turnover or unit sales. They must be linked to profits.

11 Test-market new products and services before rushing into the market.

12 Plan your marketing 'mix', gross margins and prices.

13 Plan minimum performance levels and latest dates to avoid getting too deeply into difficulties.

14 Work out a method to substantially increase demand from existing customers.

15 Examine whether you could win more of the existing market from competitors.

16 Seek out new potential market areas, for example, export markets, licensing, selling know-how, etc.

17 Regularly seek to improve your product/service.

18 Organize your salesforce effectively to maximize sales and retain incentive at a high level. Make sure that the efforts of your salespeople reflect growth and opportunity. It would be unwise to pursue a large volume of sales which attracted low profitability as against a small turnover which successfully produced higher margins.

Action Guidelines

1   Is it your intention to write a plan? If not, what are you going to do?

_____

_____

2   What are your goals in business?
      To control an empire?
      To become a millionaire?
      To run a successful business?
      To become a public company?
      To get other people to do all the work for you?
      Or what?

_____

_____

_____

3   What are your short-range plans?

_____

_____

4   What are your long-range plans?

_____

_____

5   Identify your strengths in the business.

_____

_____

6   What are your weaknesses?

_____

_____

7   Do you recognize any opportunities?

_____

_____

8 List the threats!

9 Write down the marketing 'mix' most suitable for your business.

10 What research will you do?

11 Where will you find it?

12 How are you setting your prices?

13 Explain your methods of selling and look for means of
improving them.

14 Who are your competitors and what is their market share?

_____

_____

_____

15 What is the likely life-cycle of your product/service?

_____

_____

_____

16 Can you improve or extend it?

_____

_____

_____

17 Do you have a replacement when it does expire? If so, will it be ready
    in time?

_____

_____

_____

18 Who are your customers, how many are there and where are they?

_____

_____

_____

_____

19 How do you reach them?

_____

_____

_____

_____

20 Now ,write out your marketing plan!

_____

_____

3

How to Structure Your Plan and Adapt it

- What financial information do you need?
- Do you know how to prepare it?
- How complicated should it be?
- What is the purpose of a budget?
- Did you know you can do it all yourself?
- How can you forecast without a crystal ball?
- What are your future business prospects?

Financial information

In the last unit we set out the planning process needed to identify your objectives and set your business on the right track. The information in the plan was basic to your aims because you had to make sure you knew the direction in which your business was going. You now need to fill in that framework with financial information which will show specifically what is happening. Most of the details will come to light each month, quarter, half-year, and at the end of the year. However, you will have to work out budgets and forecasts which will act as your targets, and monitor regularly whether you are matching those targets. If not, adjustments or changes will have to be made to the main plan so that you do not go too far adrift.

Most technical businessmen and non-accountants are usually

terrified of figurework. They leave it all to their accountant, if they have one. But there is no reason to feel unhappy about doing it yourself. It is not necessary to provide masterpieces – simple statements are fine. Your knowledge of balance sheets, profit and loss accounts and cash flow statements is probably remote, so here is a brief run-down on the important features, to allow you to understand why they are needed. After all, when you ask for finance from external sources (banks, institutions, the government, etc.) you are expected to provide financial figures showing your track record, if any, together with forecasts showing what you expect to happen in the future. If you do have an accountant, make sure that you are able to communicate with him or her. If not, do not be concerned – you can do it for yourself. However, if you really do not understand what needs to be done, do not do it! In such a situation, you will have to employ an accountant. First of all, let us look at the whole business function in a diagram to see how the operation works in a nutshell. You can see how the network of operations ties in to represent the full picture of your business.

Figure 2   *The business operation*

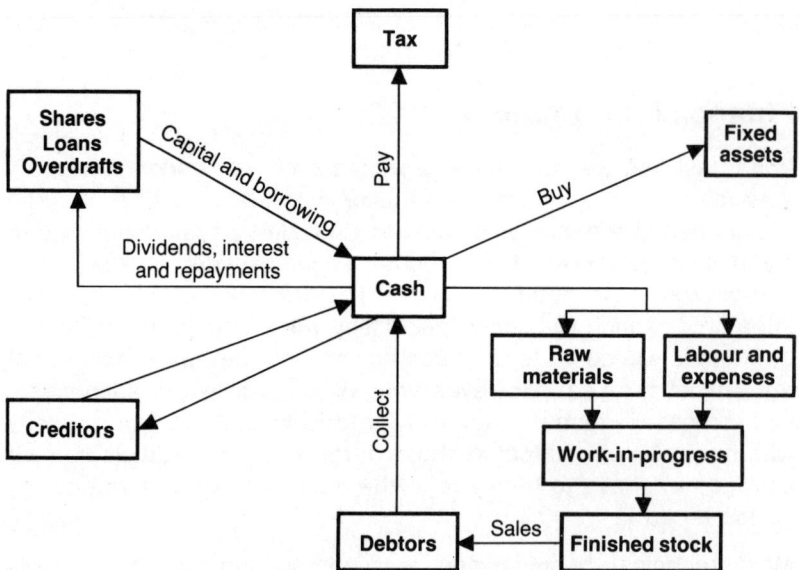

The figures you will need to produce are the balance sheet, the trading and profit and loss account, and the cash flow forecast. We shall take these one by one.

The balance sheet

The *balance sheet* is a statement of the share capital and reserves (the shareholders' investment in the business), the liabilities or debts, and the assets. This is completed on the last day of the accounting period, say 31st December. Companies with limited liability – you can buy a ready-made company for just over £100* – raise long-term finance from shareholders in the form of share issues and retained earnings; secured and unsecured long-term loans mainly from institutional investors; and short-term finance from banks, finance companies and hire-purchase companies. After raising the finance, it is invested in assets, which have a long, but limited, life in the form of buildings, plant and machinery, vehicles, etc., and also in current assets, such as stocks, debtors, cash, and so on.

Table 4   Balance sheet as at 31 December 19 . .

Liabilities	£	Assets	£
Capital	15,000	Buildings	5,000
Creditors	2,000	Plant/machinery	2,000
Bank loan	2,500	Motor vehicles	2,000
Tax	400	Stock	7,500
Dividend	100	Debtors	3,000
		Cash	500
	20,000		20,000

* Ready-made companies may be purchased from:

Express Company Registrations Ltd, Epworth House, City Road, London, EC1Y 1AA (Tel. 01 628 5434)

ICC Information Group Ltd, 38–42 Banner St, London EC1Y 8QE (Tel. 01 253 0063)

Jordan & Sons Ltd, Jordan House, 47 Brunswick Place, London, N1 6EE (Tel. 01 253 3030)

Solicitors' Law Stationery Society, 70–74 City Road, London, EC1Y 2DQ (Tel. 01 253 0444)

The example proves how easy it is to draw up a balance sheet from figures available within the files of the business.

The profit and loss account

The trading, profit and loss account shows the costs of goods manufactured during the period of the accounts, the cost of goods sold during the period of the accounts, the sales for the period, and the gross profit. The gross profit is transferred to the profit and loss account. Marketing and distribution costs, administrative costs, and any research and development expenditure are deducted to determine the company's trading or operating profit for the period. Income is then added and interest payable deducted to give profit before taxation, from which corporation tax is deducted to give the net profit or loss for the period. The example shows how simply this can be done. As you can see, the task is not at all complicated and can be carried out at any time from the figures available in the business.

Table 5 Trading, profit and loss account		
	£	£
Sales		100,000
less Purchases of raw materials	40,000	
Opening stock of raw materials	5,000	
	45,000	
Closing stock of raw materials	6,000	39,000
		61,000
Manufacturing wages	20,000	
Manufacturing overheads	5,000	25,000
		36,000
less Administration expenses	8,000	
Selling & distribution expenses	8,000	16,000
Net profit before tax and interest		20,000

Budgets

One of the very important tasks you will have to carry out is budgeting. Many businessmen turn up their noses at this point because they consider that budgets are hard work for nothing – but that is not the case at all. They are a means of helping you to assess the likely effects on your business of the decisions you take. When your business starts to grow, its problems become more difficult. Those matters you used to be able to solve by a quick decision now have to be planned. A budget is the only way you can compare your actual results with those you planned. Before we embark on what you need to do, let us first make clear the difference between budgeting and forecasting (which we shall come on to next), otherwise you may tend to confuse these issues.

A forecast is the 'best estimate' of the outcome of future trading. It is based on assumptions with an appraisal of the resources available within your business and what they will achieve. It should be distinguished from a budget, which is a 'programme of action' which management sets out to achieve. The forecast may of course form the basis of the budget.

You can prepare your budget for any period, although the most commonly used budget will be for one year, broken down month by month.

The essence of an effective budgeting system is that, having prepared your budget by forecasting your sales, cost of raw materials, labour, overheads, etc., you will check your actual figures against the budget regularly, in order to identify any large variations quickly, so that you can take whatever action you think is necessary. Your budget must be realistic if it is going to be of any value. It should be prepared extremely carefully, basing your forecasts on the past performance of your business (if any), the market demand for your products or service, and the general business environment in which you operate. If you run a very small business, you probably have to take all the decisions yourself on the level of sales, costing and pricing, materials purchases, and so on. If you run a larger business, you may employ people who are responsible for each of these functions, in which case it is essential for them to be involved in the preparation of the budget. Whatever the size of your business, the same decisions have to be taken. The items to be included in your budget are as follows:

1 *Sales*

This is one of the most important figures and requires careful thought. It will determine the expected level of activity in your business for the coming year. The following points should be considered:

(a) Past trends Your sales forecast will relate to your performance over the last few years, but it should also allow for any expansion plans or proposed diversity into a new product/service. In certain instances it may be helpful to break down the sales total into product ranges or groups of services.

(b) Market demand An assessment of the market demand for your product or service is important. For example:
Is the market expanding?
If not, is it because of changing fashions or techniques?
How strong is the competition and what is your market share? You may have difficulty in analysing this part, but it should be attempted if possible.

(c) Pricing You should consider whether your prices need to be increased during the year (allowing for inflation) and, if so, by how much and when. Remember that your price should be fixed to account not only for your costs plus a margin, but also for your judgement of the competitive price in the marketplace.

(d) Orders to date Your order books will give you an indication of likely sales for at least part of the budgeted period.

(e) Seasonality problems Resist the temptation to insert one-twelfth of total expected sales for each month of the year. There are bound to be peaks and troughs and these should be shown because they affect your cash flow.

(f) General business/economic climate The general business conditions in your industry and the likely effect of any changes in economic policy or legislation will influence your thinking concerning the sales forecast.

(g) Production capacity In a manufacturing concern it is necessary to consider production capacity in relation to the sales forecast before working out the direct materials

and labour involved. You will have to assess how much capacity is required to achieve the planned level of sales, taking into account the number of working weeks (say forty-eight weeks to allow for holidays) and your stockholding policy. Having answered this question, you can prepare a monthly estimate showing when sales have to be produced.

2 *Direct materials and labour*
The next stage is to budget for purchases of materials and labour. Your purchasing budget should include costs of both raw materials and finished goods, allowing for inflation and cost increases. Your labour (or manpower) budget will quantify the cost of labour required to achieve the production levels estimated in the budget, including wage increases expected during the year.

3 *Increase/decrease in stock*
Stock control is an essential part of financial planning for your business, not least because it can tie up a large proportion of your working capital.

4 *Gross profit*
By means of a simple deduction you can calculate your gross profit figure. An important rule of thumb is that when gross profit falls below a certain level, usually about 30 per cent, working capital requirements escalate sharply (except where a cash trade operates, when this figure would be lower). In an expanding business, it is advisable, therefore, to measure gross margins on a monthly basis.

5 *Administrative overheads*
The forecast for overheads will comprise those costs which tend to be fixed, such as office salaries, rent and rates, and those which vary in proportion to level of sales, or production, such as light, heat and power. Some of these amounts will be due quarterly or half-yearly, but it is preferable to show them on a monthly basis to prevent a distortion of the profit figure. Remember that all expenses which will affect your net profit should be included – for example, depreciation, finance charges and directors' remuneration. Conversely, any cash movements which do not affect the profit figure should be excluded – for example, capital expenditure. Capital

Table 6 Profit and loss budget for year to 31 December 19 . .

	Jan	Feb	Mar	Aprl	May	Jun	Jul	Aug	Sep	Oct	Nov	Dec	TOTAL
1 Sales	150	180	180	210	240	180	180	210	210	240	180	180	2,340
2 Direct materials	48	66	60	84	78	96	60	72	72	78	72	30	816
3 Direct labour	42	42	42	42	42	42	48	48	48	48	48	48	540
4 (Increase) decrease in stock	—	—	6	—	24	(12)	—	6	6	18	(12)	12	48
5 Cost of sales (Total of 2 3 4)	90	108	108	126	144	126	108	126	126	144	108	90	1,404
6 Gross profit (Total of 1 minus 5)	60	72	72	84	96	84	72	84	84	96	72	60	936
7 Administrative overheads	36	36	30	30	36	36	42	42	36	36	36	36	432
8 Other expenses	12	12	12	12	12	12	12	12	12	12	12	12	144
9 Net profit before tax (Total of 7 plus 8 minus 6)	12	24	30	42	48	36	18	30	36	48	24	12	360

repayments cannot be deducted before taxable profit is calculated. Value Added Tax should be excluded since it is either payable or recoverable from Customs and Excise.

6 *Net profit before tax*
After allowing for any sundry expenses, you can now calculate your net profit before tax. If you are not satisfied with this projection, remember that you can only increase your profits by:

(a) Raising prices
(b) Increasing sales volume
(c) Reducing costs
(d) Altering the product 'mix'

Budget review
You should review your budget and judge whether it compares favourably not only with your financial targets for the next twelve months but also with last year's performance. Make sure, however, that your sales forecast is not too ambitious when set against your production capacity or the availability of labour in your business.

The next step is the vital task of monitoring actual performance against budget to make sure your plans are succeeding. In this way you can identify variations quickly and, if necessary, take corrective action. This can be done long before the audited accounts are produced by your accountant – at which time (if you did not prepare budgets) your business will probably be listing like a ship taking in water.

Advantages of budgetary control
Clearly, there are some very valuable advantages to be gained from budgetary control:

- The limits prevent you from becoming extravagant, focusing your attention on costs before you decide to spend.
- You are forced to examine every resource in your business, which stops you from aiming at impractical goals.
- You co-ordinate every part of your business to achieve the objectives.

- Regular reviews will show whether you are on course, or not, and adjustments can be made fairly quickly.
- Monitoring the actual figures against your budgets will soon show whether you have been too ambitious.

But you will be wise to note some of the pitfalls which exist:

- A budget is designed to monitor progress – you should not rely on it to act as a regulator.
- You are not obliged to spend the money in a specific budget if it has not been fully used up at the end of the year.
- In times of high inflation, it is absolutely vital to review budgets regularly because changes will occur so frequently.

The main problem affecting budgetary control is that the sales forecast, on which the sales budget is prepared, cannot be accurately assessed; there are too many unpredictable factors, such as changing consumer tastes, new developments in competitors' products, and changes in the economic climate. If sales figures fluctuate widely, budgets based on fixed figures cannot operate effectively, which is the reason why budgets have to be flexible.

Forecasting

If your business is to be successful it must be both profitable and cash-generating. These two things do not always go hand in hand. Cash is a scarce resource which should be managed with care – wages and creditors cannot be paid with profits when there is no cash in the bank. If you make no attempt to forecast the outcome of trading, in profit and cash terms, your survival could be in jeopardy, because you will not know where you are going in financial terms. Forecasting requires businesses to try to predict the financial outcome of future trading, and it is a vital element of normal control procedures – you will soon find out if you are badly off target. If you are, cash will dwindle quickly and profits will fade. Therefore, you must try to get the forecast right. A full forecast consists of the following elements.

Assumptions

Assumptions must be made in every forecast. They should be produced in the form of notes since they are crucial to any forecast, and to its understanding by a third party. Assumptions must be useful; if they are vague and meaningless you are wasting your time.

Profit forecast

The aim of the profit forecast is to make the best estimate of the profit that will be derived from trading activities in the forecast period. There is little point in producing a cash forecast without first producing a profit forecast.

Cash flow forecasting

You cannot survive in business without an adequate cash flow to meet commitments to creditors and employees. A shortage of cash can raise serious problems and it is no secret that the most common cause of business failure occurs when management does not become aware of the financial situation until it is too late. Cash flow must never be confused with profits. Profits may have to be ploughed back into the business to finance a higher level of debtors or stock, but cash flow relates to cash paid into the business and cash paid out. Even highly profitable concerns can experience cash flow problems, especially if they have left an insufficient cash margin to maintain liquidity.

You must exercise strict control over cash flow and identify periods of possible cash shortage as far in advance as possible, so that you can take the appropriate steps. A cash flow forecast offers the following benefits:

- It provides an indication that sufficient cash is available to meet your trading needs throughout the coming year.
- It identifies the likely effect on liquidity of any capital investment you have planned.
- Since it facilitates the best use of cash, it can help to keep interest charges to a minimum and allow surplus funds to be invested.
- It will give you warning of a cash shortage, allowing you to arrange more finance. In such instances, the bank manager or

financial institution will want to see a copy of the forecast to discuss the basis on which your figures have been calculated.

- You will be able to monitor actual cash flow against your forecast and allocate priorities on expenditure if necessary.

Once you have prepared your profit and loss budget, you will have most of the information required to produce a cash flow forecast. Unlike the profit and loss budget, however, all cash items must be included, whether or not they affect profits. Depreciation should be left out as it does not involve cash. The following items will require consideration:

Receipts
Payments from debtors
Cash sales
Other revenue sources

Payments
Payments to creditors
Cash purchases
Wages/salaries/PAYE
Rent/rates/insurance
Light/heat/power
VAT
HP payments/leasing charges
Bank/finance charges and interest
Tax and dividend
Loan repayments
Capital expenditure

The item relating to capital expenditure is worthy of special mention. A decision to invest in new plant or machinery, etc., requires very careful thought, bearing in mind the significant effect it will have on the future prospects of your business. There are a number of methods of appraisal to help you reach a decision, but you ought to seek the advice of your accountant.

A simple cash flow forecast is set out in Table 7, and further examples are shown in Chapter 4.

Table 7 Cash flow forecast for year ended 31 December 19 ..

	Jan	Feb	Mar	Apr	May	Jun	Jul	Aug	Sep	Oct	Nov	Dec	TOTAL
Receipts													
From debtors													
Cash sales													
Total A													
Payments													
To creditors													
Overheads													
Capital expenditure													
Total B													
Net inflow A minus B													
Net outflow B minus A													
Opening Balance													
Closing Balance													

It is important to compare your cash forecast with actual results regularly, in order to ensure that cash flow is progressing to plan. However, if you experience delays in payment from one or more of your debtors you may have to seek extended credit or additional finance for a temporary period to compensate.

Sales forecast

You will need to phase the sales forecast by each month in accordance with past trading experience, rather than just spread an annual forecast equally over each month. Do not forget to forecast the expected volume of sales as well as their value. The main questions to ask are as follows:

1 What is the extent of the order book? What degree of confidence can be placed on getting more orders?

2 What is the current sales experience?

3 What is the trend of sales?

4 What monthly incidence of sales is expected? Compare it against past experience.

5 What will be the effect of competition?

6 What is the outlook for the market?

7 Are there capacity constraints on the sales forecast in:
Production?
Distribution?
Administration?

8 What effect of marketing policy is forecast?

9 What will be the effect of national economic conditions?

10 Are forecast discounts realistic?

11 Are forecast margins realistic?

12 What is the forecast effect of price rises on volume and margins?

Production costs and gross margin forecast

The forecast of gross margins resulting from the expected volume and value of sales is affected mainly by forecasts of the costs of materials, labour and factory overheads. The questions to ask are:

1 Is production capacity sufficient to meet the forecast? Is more machinery or space required?

2   How do forecast margins differ from past results?

3   Are raw material costs and labour costs being passed on?

4   Can increased raw material costs and labour costs be passed on?

5   Are raw material supplies readily available?

6   What is the basis of forecast wage increases in the period? What will be the effect?

7   Is labour readily available at the rates you want to pay?

8   Has stock wastage and obsolescence been taken into account?

9   What are the costs of increased production in:
    Bonuses?
    New manpower?
    New machinery?

10 Is existing machinery reliable?

11 Is there sufficient storage space?

12 Are productivity increases forecast, and on what basis?

13 What is the effect of a change in the sales mix on overall margins?

The overhead costs forecast
This shows the overhead costs which must be incurred in order to achieve the forecast level of sales. Inflation and the underlying levels of overheads should be taken into account, and help can be obtained in forecasting individual items by obtaining information from suppliers or by increasing overheads at the forecast inflation rate. The forecast should be consistent with the sales/production forecast; for example, many overhead items (commissions, postage, transport, telephone costs) will rise with an increased volume of sales.

A statement of financial facilities
This is useful if finance has been sought. It should include details of facilities, security arrangements, repayment terms and rates, so that you can understand your financial position at a glance.

Summary

A forecast can only be considered to be properly prepared if all aspects of your business have been taken into account. For example, if sales are the main constraint on the achievement of a forecast, and if these are forecast to double in a year, then the effects must be reflected in:

The capacity of the factory
The sales team
Transport
Storage
Administration
Advertising and promotion costs
Margins
Working capital
Service improvement

Full account should be taken of inflation at rates appropriate to the business, and the assumptions used should be explained clearly.

If you are honest with yourself, you will admit that preparing financial information is not really half as difficult as you thought. We have covered most of it step-by-step, and you should now realize that you do not need to be a financial genius or an accountant to do the job – you can do it yourself, and you should do it regularly.

What we have done is to build the skeleton of a successful business operation – the business plan – and we have filled in the rest with budgets and forecasts which give us the complete picture. One of the main advantages is that you can prepare your financial information at any time – that is, the actual figures – and compare them with your budget. If things are going adrift, you can see the problem immediately, and then do something about if. If you adopt the planning and budgeting procedures, you will feel that you have a high degree of control over everything that happens, which should cause you less concern. Almost certainly the right plan and the proper controls should allow you to grow quickly and properly.

Action Guidelines

1 Draw up a specimen balance sheet for your business as it stands today.

_____

_____

_____

_____

2 Prepare also a specimen trading and profit and loss account.

_____

_____

_____

_____

3 Devise a sales budget consisting of past trends, market demand, pricing, orders to date, seasonality problems, the business/economic climate, and production capacity.

_____

_____

_____

_____

4 Analyse budget information on direct materials and labour, increase/decrease in stock, gross profit, administrative overheads and net profit before tax.

_____

_____

_____

_____

5 What are the advantages of budgetary control?

_____

_____

6   What will forecasting do for your business?

_____

_____

_____

_____

7   Why is a cash flow forecast so useful?

_____

_____

_____

_____

8   Prepare an outline cash flow forecast.

_____

_____

_____

_____

9   Work out what happens to your cash flow if you increase sales by
    20 per cent.

_____

_____

_____

_____

10 Explaining your assumptions, prepare:
    A sales forecast
    A production costs/gross margins forecast
    An overhead costs forecast

11 Produce a statement of financial facilities which includes details of facilities, security, repayment terms and rates.

12 Using your budgets for this year, how close are your forecasts in relation to future trading prospects, comparing cash, assets, stock, sales, production costs, etc?

4

How to Present Your Plan

- What is the lender looking for?
- How can you convince a financier to lend you money?
- Is your company worth lending money to?
- What are the key features of a proposal?
- What do you have to do to succeed in getting finance?
- Will you be able to do it successfully yourself?
- How do you do your own cash flow forecast?

There are few businesses which are so flush with funds that they do not need to borrow money – such firms are a very rare breed! If you examine the accounts of most major companies, you will see that they all borrow large sums of money. The reasons are varied depending on their operations, but the amounts that they borrow are enormous! So why should you stand on the sidelines worrying about borrowing money, whether you are established or just starting-up with a new product or service? In effect, if you can present a good case and succeed in getting finance, you will benefit by developing your business plans, and the lender will benefit by the amount of interest earned on the loan.

The trouble is that lending money is such a risky business. Sometimes there are no problems at all; at other times, even though the proposition may seem sound and the prospects bright, unforeseen circumstances crop up which change the whole pattern, and the loan may never be repaid. In the light of this uncertainty, and in the knowledge that a lender will be very cautious, how can you convince someone else to part with money for your business? Answer – you have to do some simple research and follow a formal plan. If you want to succeed you have to know what is in the mind of the other person when you ask for money, and what they are looking for. Then you need to set to work to let them know that you really understand your business, at the same time showing any spark of commercial brilliance you have to help you. There are two things to consider at this particular moment. Firstly, with all the risks, competition, problems and difficulties relating to your business at the present time, if you were standing in the shoes of a potential lender would you risk offering money to your business? Be honest! If the answer is on the downside you will probably have to work harder on your proposal. If it is positive, do not be misled into thinking that the lender should be honoured to let you have the money. The system does not work that way. Secondly, if you believe that you are a good risk, can you identify what the lender wants to know? After all, if you are able to do that properly you could be halfway to becoming a Marks & Spencer or an ICI. If you are a good businessman you will dedicate yourself to the effort. The process is not really difficult at all, and the information set out below takes you step-by-step through the procedure.

Before starting on that journey, however, let us assess a few of the elementary points you need to consider. The proposal must be reasonable, with good future prospects. It would be time-wasting, for example, for a barrow boy with one barrow to try to borrow half a million pounds to expand his business. He might argue that he would install pitches at markets all over the country, but the lender would hardly be convinced. Applications are carefully assessed in terms of the product or service offered, its market strengths and the quality of the management. In addition, you are expected to have commercial as well as technological ability (although the loan does not necessarily depend on this factor), and you should have made a real commitment to the venture with your own finance and time. It is no good having put up a thousand pounds in a venture as an investment, and then devoting the main part of your time to another business elsewhere. You and your associates, partners, directors or backers have to be deeply involved!

There is no precise pattern for proposals because each business varies so much, but you will always be expected to make a thorough presentation. This would be set out in the style shown below, but lending institutions are usually prepared to interpret matters flexibly. Before that, however, you should have a realistic idea of how much you are prepared to concede in fees and commission, interest rates, and equity in the business, and work out how much security is available. Although many loans are granted without security, it is of little use attempting to arrange a substantial loan if the security you have available falls far short of the amount requested. The lender must be presumed to require full coverage by means of security. If the amount of security available falls short of the finance you wish to borrow, your proposal is bound to fail, unless the lender is willing to accept the risk.

Arranging a meeting

The very first step is to arrange a meeting with your bank manager or the financial institution to discuss your financial needs and your plans. This is so much wiser than dumping a presentation on the lender's lap in the hope that funds will come through fairly quickly. If you meet first the lender will be able to make certain suggestions giving you useful clues for the presentation content, and there will be an awareness of your needs. It is important that you take profit and loss, cash flow forecasts and balance sheet figures with you at the initial interview, to allow a general assessment to be made of your business and to improve your chances in getting the finance you want. The lender may also suggest the kinds of finance best suited to your plans, and you could submit your proposal knowing that both you and the lender are of one mind. It is possible that you may be charged for the interview, but if you arrange the interview with a Small Firms Centre, CoSIRA, or a Local Enterprise Agency (see Unit 7) it will be free.

There is one other problem you should consider very carefully. Lenders are usually in great demand and they can pick and choose which proposals they prefer to accept. Hence, your proposal to the lending institution is a 'once only' effort. Banks and financial institutions do not normally return proposals with suggested amendments, and it is only on very rare occasions that you will receive it back for redrafting, return and another look. The proposal is approved on the information presented at the time or it is turned down. And because so few business people know what they need to do, or how to do it properly, a very large number of applications are rejected every day.

What the lender is looking for

We started with the fact that lending is a very risky venture for the financier, and we come to the conclusion that borrowing is an extremely serious matter for the business person. The next step is to find out what goes on inside the mind of a lender, in order to understand what is required from you when you ask for money. The following points are extremely important and should help you.

Character	Your personal honesty and integrity is not enough in itself. A track record of sound business operation and creditworthiness over a period of years is far more important.
Ability	The results of business activity must show that you are very capable, with sufficient skill to run a business properly in both good and bad economic times.
Capital	You are expected to provide substantial credit yourself. A lender will assess the private means of partners and traders because they are fully liable for their firm's debts; the directors of small limited companies will be asked to give personal guarantees and to provide details of directors' loans to the company at regular intervals.
Connections	You may have fairly influential friends with accounts at your bank, or members of your family may have healthy bank balances there. A bank manager would be very concerned at the risk of losing their business if your application was refused. You may do well to trade on known connections.

Security	The taking of security will never turn a bad advance into a good one. Security is taken as cover against loss in the event of unforeseen circumstances which may prevent you from repaying the loan.

There is nothing devious in these key items, but that is not the end of it because the lender then has the task of asking certain other vital questions:

- **Who is the customer?** Are you old-established, a new business, or do you wish to transfer the account from another bank which has probably already refused a loan? What is your track record and that of the business?
- **Why is the money needed?** Will the funds be used for a definite purpose relating to the growth or development of the business, and not to finance deficits caused by poor trading?
- **What will the money be used for?** There are a variety of reasons: to buy plant and machinery, to buy new premises, a takeover, working capital, etc.
- **How much is needed?** Too many proposers have only a vague idea of how much they want to borrow, or they ask for a limited amount which they think the bank or institution would be happy to lend. Such attitudes may place a business in extreme danger and they are very unwise. It is far better to ask for more than is required, so that some funds will be available for unexpected additional costs. You really cannot keep going back to ask for a little bit more very time a problem occurs.
- **When will the advance be paid?** The lender will want the return of the money over a period of time, plus interest. He does not expect to lend on a long-term basis unless agreement is specified.
- **Where will repayment come from?** It is not enough to suggest that repayments of the loan will probably come through growth after the loan is granted. You will need to prove that the loan will secure growth or development which will generate funds sufficient to repay the loan.

In a nutshell, the lender is looking to invest in a sound business with potential growth and development. It needs to be run by a capable business person with a good track record who has invested a fair amount of his or her capital into the business and can offer security for any required loans. Information is also needed concerning the reasons for the request, the use the funds will be put to, and repayments.

These features hardly sound formidable – but how can you prove them to a lender? You may have little trouble in establishing your ability, by virtue of a good track record. But that element is not enough on its own. As mentioned earlier, applications are rarely returned for amendment if they fail to match the requirements of the bank or institution – especially with small businesses. It is a 'rifle shot' approach, which needs to be accurate and absolutely on target. If the amount of finance required is very low it may be approved by the local bank manager by word of mouth. A large loan will almost certainly need approval by senior management. Hence, a written proposal will have to be prepared in a well reasoned and clearly presented form. This is probably your one-and-only chance; if it fails, you may have to approach another bank or financial institution and start all over again. The result is a loss of valuable time and effort, apart from delaying your future plans. So, together, we have to get it right first time. But before moving to the next stage which seems like hard work, let us look at the task that lies ahead, and examine the key features which make up the proposal that you will complete and present in due course.

Key features of the application

Brief summary of the proposal	● How much money is needed? ● Why is it needed? ● What will it be used for? ● What is the likely outcome?
History of the business (if it has been trading)	● When did it start? ● What does it do? ● How has it developed? ● Location ● Other significant details

Activities of the business	• What is the general nature of the business? • The number of branches/outlets/depots • The product/service range • Market share • Main competitors • Sales/profit analysis by product/service • Sales analysis by main customers • Exports: turnover and countries
Production facilities (if the business produces goods)	• Details of products • Production volumes and capacity • Age and type of plant and machinery • Product life-cycles • New products • Competitive advantages • Annual expenditure on research and development • Seasonal aspects
Service capability (if the business offers a service)	• Details of the service • Extent of floorspace (in retailing) • Customer levels • Competitive advantages • New service features • Seasonal aspects
Markets and marketing	• Geographic coverage • Customer identification • Marketing and promotional strategy • Pricing • New markets • Distribution

Management and structure	<ul><li>Details of directors and their interests</li><li>Group structure and other company connections</li><li>Management structure and division of responsibilities of senior executives</li><li>Number of employees in each main area of business</li><li>Trade union representation and the state of industrial relations</li><li>The relevance to the local economy and employment of any planned investment</li></ul>
Audited accounts	<ul><li>Balance sheets (three years)</li><li>Profit and loss accounts (three years)</li></ul>
Borrowing limits	<ul><li>What is the maximum forecast borrowing identified against borrowing limits laid down in the articles of association (if a limited company)?</li></ul>
The finance and its purpose	<ul><li>What is the amount of money needed?</li><li>What will the money be used for?</li><li>What are the benefits expected by the business if the finance is granted?</li><li>What will be the method and timing of repayment?</li><li>Where will repayment come from?</li></ul>
Cash projections	<ul><li>Projections showing the impact of the proposed financing.</li></ul>

Security	• What type(s) of security are available?
	• Details of marketability
	• Details of market value
Existing financial and other arrangements	• What is your present bank and branch?
	• Details of overdraft, loans and other banking or institutional services
	• Details of stockbrokers, registrars, solicitors, consultants, etc.

Before you flinch from having further involvement in this mammoth task, let us examine each detail separately. It may look horrifying and very time-consuming to tackle, especially if you have little time to spare because of the many hours spent in keeping the business going. But that is not necessarily the case. The second wave of concern, no doubt, will be that the job requires the help of a professional person in accounting and marketing. That is not necessarily the case either. You can do it yourself without too much difficulty, and you will find it relatively easy to follow a simple pattern. But first, we must face reality. There is a strong possibility that you have read these points and decided that many of them do not fit in with your operations. Needless to say, they have been designed to cover every eventuality and you will need to make adjustments to fit your business in particular. However, do not delude yourself that you can cunningly miss out a lot of them merely because you do not want to get involved in too much work. We are not dealing here with choice but with the need to respond to a bank or financial institution with those answers which they seek. Hence, you need to adjust the template accordingly and set to work.

Let us look at each item carefully. If, at the end of it, you decide that the whole thing is impossible, you will have two options: one is to read the text over again and let the reasoning sink in; the other is to look for a job somewhere else because you are not the business-man you thought you were!

The brief summary
Before wading through pages of text, the bank manager or institutional lender will want to know what the proposal is all about. This summary offers the opportunity to recognize and understand what is needed and its purpose. What will be explained in this part is the development policy of the business: how much you need to borrow to pursue it; how the money will be used; and what the likely outcome will be if the finance is provided. The business should have a successful and expanding record, or good potential, with which to support its application. In newly formed businesses there must be real potential for growth or development. Unless supported by on-going operations, it is expected that new products should normally have been developed to the stage where commercial exploitation can start, with evidence of a demand for the product. Specific reasons for seeking finance are usually related to investment such as plant and machinery, a takeover, to meet a seasonal trading peak, to increase working capital generally, for short or medium-term borrowing (which may include buying a property or a factory), to enlarge the trading base of your business, or to improve the balance sheet position. As a guide to length, the summary should not exceed 1200 words.

History of the business
This section is a thumbnail sketch of the business from the time it first began to trade to the present day. If your business is just starting from scratch, this part of the proposal cannot be completed in depth. In such cases, greater emphasis will need to be placed on the product or service and its potential. An established business will need to identify the year it started, with a review of how it has developed over the years to the present time. This should be enhanced by brief details of growth in turnover, profits, staff, outlets/depots, markets, details of product or service development, and details of policy. You should include information on location, and a description of the buildings occupied by the business, stating whether they are freehold or leasehold, together with any other significant details.

Activities of the business

This part of the exercise is usually considered one of the easiest, for it concerns the day-to-day operation, of which you are most aware. The product involved may be clothing, batteries, motor cars or chocolate. The service could be transport, contract cleaning, retailing, or some other activity in the industrial, commercial or leisure environment. It may well be that the business operates in two or more types of commercial activities, in which case they should be clearly defined in the proposal. In addition, a sales and profit analysis for each product or service should be set out with the percentage of sales and profit allocated for each area of operation.

Next comes the number of branches/outlets/depots and their geographical location, followed by details of the range of the product or service, and how it meets the needs of the industry or the consumer. If it is possible to identify the market share of your business it should be given, but many businesses are too small to have any impact at all. The details should also show the major competitors and their market share. Further information on competitors should be given in relation to the activities of the business, and any other relevant material available ought to be added.

The main customers of the business should be mentioned. Sometimes they are major companies which may lend some weight to the proposal. Whether they are or not, they should be listed, with the turnover of each individual customer, because the lender will want to know if only a few companies provide most of the sales. The great danger here is that if a business has only three main customers and one of them decided to trade elsewhere, or terminate that particular line of activity, the effect on your business could be catastrophic. There is a great deal of safety in having many small customers rather than a few large ones, and the lender will be looking for such information.

The business may be involved in exporting worldwide or to a few specific countries. Details on sales in the UK and other countries should be set out in order to offer a clear picture to the lender.

Production facilities (if producing goods)

You should submit specific details of products, whether they are still being developed or not, in order to allow the lender to appraise the potential market and the products' value to industry and the community. Production volumes will indicate capacity and output and signify whether the business can increase its production to allow for the expansion for which the finance is needed. The age of major plant and machinery should be shown to ascertain if it is becoming obsolete, if it is old or if it is fairly new.

Of particular importance is the matter of life-cycles. The life of each product starts with demand but it is overtaken eventually by changes in fashion, more modern products or competition. When life-cycles start to fall some way past their peak, the finance requested might be required to prop up falling sales. A lender will want to see that this is not the case.

An outline with technical details of new products will strengthen the proposal, and details of competitive advantages will make it clear whether the products will have a chance of succeeding. In addition, the amount of annual expenditure on research and development over the past three years, if any has been undertaken, should be shown.

Service capability (if offering a service)
The service should be explained carefully so that there can be no misinterpretation. A proposal for finance relating to warm-air hand-dryers installed in washrooms was rejected because the bank manager could not understand the use of the machine as a result of the technical jargon in the submission. Another proposal to set up a group of massage parlours was turned down because the information kept mentioning the beautiful girls who would be employed, and all the additional services they would offer beyond those of competitors. The bank manager was concerned that he might be lending for immoral purposes.

In the retail trade, it would be helpful to assess the extent of the floor space and shelving, as well as potential development, and, whatever the service, customer levels should be mentioned. These should explain how many customers are served and the potential market in each area.

Details of competitive advantages would assist the proposal, and new service features should be made clear, with an assessment of their potential success in terms of customers and sales. Seasonal aspects are very important. Farming is most obvious in this way because there is a long lapse between seeding time and the sale of crops grown and harvested from those seeds, but there are other types of businéss with acute seasonal problems.

Markets and marketing

Geographic coverage sets out areas of operation by town, country or region. It is a means of identifying the geographic extent of business operations and the strength or weakness of sales in each area. Customer identification pinpoints the number of customers served in each area or location and the types of customers; for example, female only, classification A on the socio-economic scale (doctors, barristers, etc.) or C1s (skilled workers); or, on the industry side, breweries, dry cleaners, newspaper shops, and so on.

The marketing strategy is concerned with identifying opportunities to serve target markets on a profitable basis and to prevent competitors taking away business. The promotional strategy communicates products or services to the marketplace by means of advertising in the press, in journals, on radio, on television, by direct mail, on posters, on packaging, etc.

Pricing is of high priority, for the profits made by any business depend on the margins earned on goods, which have to be maintained against competitors. Very few small businesses can survive a price-cutting war for a long period of time. Therefore, the pricing policy and margins earned on each product or service should be included. It would be helpful to list new markets which are likely to become available in the UK or abroad, and details of distribution and operation channels also need to be shown.

Management and structure

Giving details of directors and their interests, showing their functions, qualifications, ages and experience, is an easy task, while group structure for a small business should create no problem. There may be other company connections – even perhaps a parent holding company – and it is vital that this information is included. Management structure and division of responsibilities of senior executives may not be necessary if the business is small, and the number of employees may be too low to warrant division into areas of business. Trade union representation could be important, while the relevance to the local economy and employment situation of any planned investment may have a great bearing on the outcome of the proposal, and also attract government support.

Audited accounts

Your accountant will give you balance sheets covering the three previous years, and profit and loss accounts for the same periods. You should also prepare a sales forecast to show business expectations for the next year. This should be set out as shown in Table 8.

Your accountant may consider other budget information should be submitted, although the cash flow projection set out in Table 9 ought to be sufficient.

Borrowing limits

This item is simply copied from the articles of association (if you are a limited company) to indicate that the funds requested in the proposals lie within the legal limit which the company is allowed to borrow. A partnership may have some limitation in the partnership agreement, but other traders are not fettered in this way.

The finance and its purpose

Details should be full, asking for a specific amount of money and stating the purpose for which it will be used. The benefits expected by the business are a most crucial feature and they should indicate that the finance granted will generate sufficient profits to repay the loan.

Cash projections

A cash flow forecast is a plan of the income and expenditure expected in a business. It assists you in planning ahead and in monitoring progress. Cash flow projections should be prepared for the next two years, assuming that the finance will be granted. The projections should be worked through in reasonable detail based on assumptions which are both realistic and clearly stated. This task usually horrifies most businesspeople but it is very easy – even if you have little aptitude for accountancy. Let us start off with the simple example shown in Table 9.

Table 8 Sales forecast

	This year (£)	Next year (£)
Orders received *less* cancellations	374,250	422,556
Net sales	422,070	446,352
Orders on hand at close	108,000	143,844
Net sales *plus* closing stocks of finished goods and work-in-progress, *less* opening stocks and work-in-progress	419,304	445,524
Labour		
Materials	202,500	227,958
Direct charges		
Gross profit	216,804	217,566
Salaries & indirect labour ⎫		
Other operating expenses ⎬	130,554	109,626
Depreciation ⎭		
Operating profit	86,250	107,940
Miscellaneous income *less* expenditure	(8,574)	(4,632)
Pre-tax profit	77,676	103,308

All you need to do is to list all receipts and payments and fill in estimates on a monthly basis over the next twenty-four months (see Table 9). You start with initial cash, which may be in credit or overdrawn, and end the month with a cash increase or decrease. Subtract the initial cash at the top from the cash increase or decrease at the bottom and that amount is your balance or overdraft for the end of the month. The following month this amount is moved to the top as your starting balance. For example, at the end of January the overdraft is £2,690 and, if you look at the top, that is the amount with which you start in February, and so on throughout the year. It is the very bottom line which is most important, however, for the amounts shown there are your credit balance or overdraft. If you wish to introduce a new product, the estimates might involve a lot of guesswork. Nevertheless, the cash flow forecast must be prepared.

Table 9 Specimen cash flow forecast

	Jan £	Feb £	Mar £	Apr £	May £	June £
Initial cash	4,750	(2,690)	(2,390)	830	1,780	(1,620)
Receipts						
Trade debtors	20,000	22,000	21,000	19,000	18,000	19,000
Sale of assets	1,500	—	—	—	200	—
Other	60	—	120	50	—	100
TOTAL	21,560	22,000	21,120	19,050	18,200	19,100
Payments						
Trade creditors	4,000	3,500	3,000	3,200	2,800	3,000
Other creditors	500	800	500	1,000	700	800
Wages & salaries	11,000	11,000	11,000	11,200	11,200	11,200
Heat, light & power	500	200	200	500	200	200
Advertising	—	2,000	—	—	2,000	—
Rates	2,000	—	—	—	—	—
Other expenses	1,000	2,700	2,700	1,000	2,700	2,700
Loan interest	—	—	500	—	—	—
Tax	10,000	—	—	—	—	—
Dividends	—	—	—	1,200	—	—
Capital outlay	—	1,500	—	—	2,000	—
TOTAL	29,000	21,700	17,900	18,100	21,600	17,900
Cash increase (decrease)	(7,440)	300	3,200	950	(3,400)	1,200
Credit balance (overdraft)	(2,690)	(2,390)	830	1,780	(1,620)	(420)

Table 10 Cash flow forecast for XYZ & Co.

	Enter month/quarter				
Income					
Cash sales					
Debtors					
Other revenue sources					
TOTAL INCOME FOR PERIOD	A				
OPENING BANK BALANCE					
(if in credit)					
Total	B				
Expenditure					
Cash purchase					
Creditors					
Wages/salaries					
Repairs/renewals					
Insurance					
Telephone					
Rent/rates					
Light, heat & power					
Transport, packaging					
Bank/finance charges & interest					
HP payments/leasing					
Sundry expenses					
VAT (net)					
Tax					
Dividends					
Principals' drawings					
Loan repayments					

TOTAL EXPENDITURE FOR PERIOD		
OPENING BANK BALANCE (if in debit)	C	
B minus C =	D	
	E	

E = B minus D, and the balance is carried forward to the column marked A if it is in credit or to column C if in debit.

89

The next stage is to examine the form which is used by bank managers for cash flow forecasting, so that we can see how they would like to see it. See Table 10. The notes on the form are set out as follows:

1 Decide whether monthly or quarterly figures are to be projected and head the top line accordingly.

2 Enter the bank balance in A if in credit, or C if in debit. This is the balance at the bank – not in the books of your business.

3 Income/expenditure includes all items which will pass through the bank account.

4 Items which do not pass through the bank account can be summarized overleaf.

Security
It is not necessary for you to include details of security available, but it is almost certain that you will be asked for it, so you should prepare some information in advance. Security comprises stocks and shares, guarantees, life policies, and land and buildings. Any security offered must have marketability – it must be easy to sell at any time. Problems occur when a share certificate becomes worthless on the liquidation of a company, or when property falls below the value at which the security was accepted because of subsidence, planning problems (such as the building of a motorway close by), or disrepair. Therefore, you should carry out your assessments carefully to determine what you have in the way of security and what you are prepared to release.

Existing financial and other arrangements
You should give details of the bank and branch at which the business maintains its accounts, and any other banks or merchant banks involved. Overdrafts, loans and other financial services need to be submitted. They often indicate a positive attitude to banking operations and, unless they are too complex, they show that you have been involved in establishing a sound financial base. Other details concern advisers, registrars, stockbrokers, auditors, solicitors, etc.

Conclusion
The information required does not always fall simply into the sections listed above. If that is the case, it does not matter particularly as long

as you are able to present the details in a meaningful form. All the data must be included; the way you do it depends on the type of business you run and the information available. The pattern set out here is only a template which acts as a guide for you to follow. Try not to leave anything out. Lenders survive by their ability to select good risks; they know all the ins and outs and the shortcuts. If you do not enter relevant details they will be bound to ask you for them, and that might prove embarrassing. If they do not ask, then your proposal may have failed because of it. Finally, make sure that your application is well presented. Some potential borrowers 'dump' a group of loose pages held by a single paper clip on a bank manager's desk. Not good enough! Your presentation should be smart, attractive, bound with covers, and typed on good quality stationery.

What happens next?

If the bank or institution is interested in the proposal, what happens next? Well, there are two possibilities following a successful application. In the case of most banks, a loan is granted over a specific period of time, or an overdraft limit is extended which means that you can borrow on a day-to-day basis up to the extent of the limit. As a result, you will have achieved your aim and can develop your business according to plan. The proposal may be more complicated, however, and you will probably have to attend a meeting to discuss matters in detail. Certainly, other kinds of financial institutions will ask to meet the proposer at a place convenient to both of them. It would not be unusual for a bank manager to go to your business premises and spend some time reviewing the plant and machinery and the operations; a financial institution will always do so – though reviews will always be carried out with your full knowledge and co-operation.

If the review proves favourable, a formal offer of investment will be sent. It is likely to be simple and easy to understand, outlining all the terms for acceptance. Perhaps it should be stated that, just because the bank or finance institution has made the offer, you are not obliged to accept it. The document merely indicates the offer of finance, stating the terms. The normal reaction is to sign the forms, take the money and put it to work. By this swift action time-wastage is eliminated. Right? No! Wrong! You are expected to discuss the offer with your professional advisers and then return to the lenders.

Among the conditions and restrictions that may be incorporated into any agreement by a lender or investor are some very nasty features. For example:

- Limitations on the amount the firm may borrow, secured or unsecured; or undertakings that certain specified ratios will be maintained which could cause a great deal of concern at some future time.
- A prohibition on the creation of any further charges on the assets of the business.
- Limitations on the amount of remuneration that the directors may draw, and on dividends; and continuance of existing directors' loans to the business.
- The right of the lender to monitor the performance of the business and to receive regular financial information.
- The right of the investor or lender to appoint a director to the board in the case of an equity investment.
- The right to be consulted about specific developments or unusual transactions.

Lenders are normally prepared to offer advice to applicants and can revise or modify their requirements to meet changed conditions.

Up to this point you may not have been committed to pay any costs, or fees. On acceptance however, solicitors to the bank or institution will translate the offer letter into the necessary legal documentation. Banks often produce standard forms which may be modified easily, but this might not always be the case. Commitment or whole facility fees will probably be set which could amount to 5 per cent per annum of the loan. This is a fee to the bank for setting aside the funds. Arrangement fees might be charged which relate to a simple fee to compensate for the manager's time in arranging the loan. Both commitment and arrangement fees are negotiable and, in some cases, may be eliminated altogether. In addition, you will have to pay for the cost of solicitors, accountants and other professional work involved, if there is any. And lastly, there may be a non-utilization fee charged by banks – but rarely financial institutions. If you decide not to go ahead, and the bank considers it has offered advice and spent valuable time on the proposal, it may require payment for its services. Hence, if you approach a number of banks and financial institutions with the same proposal, in order to speed up matters by giving everyone the opportunity to lend to you, your efforts may turn out to be very expensive.

Timing of applications

Fairly small loans which lie within the authority of a bank manager may be granted immediately. Security may have to be lodged, but the form filling and procedures will be short. Larger loans or financial packages require close examination, and a ruling from senior executives or committees may take considerable time. Because of the need for careful investigation and the preparation of the necessary documents and agreements, the time-scale for obtaining long-term finance can be up to three months in many cases. Therefore, it is advisable for you to plan your financial requirements well in advance, and make the necessary approach to a bank or financial institution some months before the money is likely to be needed. In any event, an approach in good time is important in making a favourable impression.

The pitfall which lies waiting for many businesses when they seek to borrow funds is the failure to provide full details to the lender. This usually stems not from a lack of detailed knowledge, but rather from not appreciating that such knowledge is not shared by the lender and must be communicated to him. Each lending situation placed before a banker is judged on its own merits. The businessman is often unaware of the method of appraisal employed and does not always present the case to his advantage. It should never be thought that the skilful presentation of a bad case will turn it into a good one. On the other hand, the bad presentation of an acceptable case can create a lack of confidence which may lead to an unsuccessful outcome.

Action Guidelines

1   Arrange an interview with your bank or financial institution to discuss your business proposition.

_____

_____

_____

2   Find out whether you have any relatives, friends or associates with good banking connections.

_____

_____

_____

3   Check the security you are willing to offer. Is it enough? Is it worth what you think it is worth? Is it marketable?

_____

_____

_____

4   Can you give good reasons why you need money – or is to finance deficits caused by poor trading?

_____

_____

_____

5   Work out how much you need.

_____

_____

_____

6   Work out how much more you need if an emergency occurs!

_____

_____

_____

7   Decide the period of the loan according to your profit expectation.

_____

_____

_____

94

8   Identify carefully how profit will emerge to repay the loan.

_____

_____

_____

9   Go back to the key features of the application and answer all the
     points in the details column .

_____

_____

_____

10   Ask your accountant to provide you with balance sheets and profit
     and loss accounts for the last three years, if you cannot find them.

_____

_____

_____

11   Prepare a sales forecast for the next twelve months.

_____

_____

_____

12   Prepare a cash flow forecast for the next twelve months.

_____

_____

_____

13   Put your whole presentation together and ask your accountant to
     check it through.

_____

_____

_____

_____

_____

_____

_____

_____

5
Do-It-Yourself Finance

- Do you know there is spare money in your business?
- Would you like to find it rather than borrow?
- What can be done with money except bank it?
- Can you ease the headache of getting people to pay you?
- Is there a way of stopping cash from flowing out?
- Does 20 per cent of your stock earn 80 per cent of your sales?
- Should you take trade discounts, or offer them, or what?
- How can your business survive in an emergency?

You may think it impossible to get money from your business without going to the bank manager or a financial institution for finance, especially when you are short of cash. Yet there are ways in which it can be done, and if you follow the steps set out below you will find out that not only does it work but you will improve your business efficiency at the same time. One of your main problems is that you have no time to spare to draw up a plan of action because of the busy day-to-day running of your business. If that is the case, let us start step-by-step with a nine-point plan which will help you to find money in your business rather than go cap-in-hand to borrow it from someone else. You *can* do it yourself.

Working capital

Your business might be struggling simply because you have not figured out your working capital properly or because you did not realize what would happen when growth began. When you start selling more goods, more working capital is wanted. This is because you need more stock – which costs money – and, if you are selling on credit, there will be more debtors owing you money. If you are experienced in the business, you may have a rule of thumb measure that working capital has to be, say, 15 per cent of sales – or there may be industry or trade association figures which offer you a guideline. The problem is that as trade increases and your sales go up, the working capital needed increases. It follows also that if your business is seasonal it will vary widely at certain times, and you must take that into account or else you will always be under financial pressure. Let us look at the working capital of a toy manufacturer whose main sales occur before Christmas, and most of the year is spent building up stock.

Table 11				
	Jan 31 £	Apr 30 £	Jul 31 £	Oct 31 £
Stock	3,600	6,300	9,000	900
plus Debtors	—	—	—	10,800
minus Creditors	(900)	(900)	(900)	(900)
equals Working capital	2,700	5,400	8,100	10,800

The working capital needed is £10,800, the peak being reached when all the year's production has been sold but none of the customers have yet paid up. In practice, the toy manufacturer will get an overdraft from the bank up to a maximum of, say, £12,000, that is the forecast of £10,800 plus £1200 for emergencies. He will not need to borrow £10,800 all the time, but he should never start production without knowing or estimating that the working capital needed is likely to be in the region of £10,800.

There are other ways of improving your working capital without using earnings as your measure. For example, you may be thinking of starting a new major project or buying plant or equipment. If the project cannot produce earnings quickly you ought to consider having another look at the idea, and even shelving it. There is no point in starting a new venture unless it can be successful within a reasonable amount of time. Do not gamble by trying to become a big business too quickly. The failure of such a project could set you back for years. If you need plant or equipment, you can get them without having to pay out cash or borrow the funds elsewhere. There are other methods such as hire purchase or leasing, where smaller payments can be made monthly or quarterly, instead of a large amount of cash which is paid when you buy the goods outright.

You could also improve the business by leaving more money in it yourself. Naturally, at first, this view will go against the grain. It is a personal sacrifice, but if you think the business is worth it, the idea should be explored. Another source of money is the use of the funds which are represented by depreciation charges. These may be used until you need to replace the machinery or asset, and your accountant can help by giving you advice on this matter. Further thought should be given to the amount of work-in-progress which can be reduced by quicker deliveries, while the length of time of some production runs may be changed to produce work faster. Any means which shortens the time between the receipt of goods/ materials and their sale will benefit your business by improving the working capital. Have another look at the way you operate – there is always a better way of doing things if you can work it out!

Trade credit

The use of trade credit and its management is a very important part of your business. As a small firm, you may find that you provide a lot of credit to the big firms in industry. In real life, large companies exercise their economic power over their smaller customers and suppliers. The threat of losing crucial supplies and orders may often force you to pay promptly, but when the tables are turned you find you have to wait patiently in line for your own accounts to be paid. There may be no immediate answer to this problem but it is up to you to make sure that all your credit affairs are managed properly. All too often this is not the case. Relying on trade credit is in many ways a risky method of financing your business. If you cannot sell the stock eventually you will have financial problems and they could prove to be expensive – especially when the loss of cash discount is considered. In some cases, where the time lag between buying raw materials/components and the sale of the finished article involves a large amount of finance, suppliers in industries are willing to extend long-term credit or offer other forms of assistance on a pre-arranged basis. For example, the engineering industry has developed the 'free issue materials' system under which the customer provides the manufacturer with the materials free of charge and pays only the costs of manufacture. Where a large company is the customer of a small one, the large firm may make an advance or loan to the small firm to buy materials and get repaid as the finished products are delivered. Another system allows help to be given towards the cost of tooling for special contracts.

In retailing, discounts are earned by joining other small retailers in special groups which are then able to buy in bulk and compete pricewise with major companies. In the toy industry, retailers are allowed to order goods to build up stocks, and sometimes free credit is allowed for a period of up to three years. There are many other such arrangements and you should contact your industry or trade association to find out what is on offer for your business.

Let us take a look now at some of the main features of trade credit:

1 Try to negotiate as much credit as possible. You should give the impression to your supplier that with a little extra help now you could become one of his major customers in the future. The personal touch is essential because you are relying on goodwill. He may insist on doing business on a 'cash only' basis. If so, you will have to go along with this for a while, but start pressing for a date when you can operate on a credit basis as soon as it is reasonable to do so.

2 Take exactly the credit you have negotiated and no more. It is in your interest to be seen as a person of your word. You want to build up good trade references as an honest businessman as quickly as possible.

3 Pay all your official creditors, that is, gas, telephone, electricity, Inland Revenue, etc., on the due date and no earlier.

4 Run a diary system to remind you when bills are due for settlement.

5 Run a system to control your debtors (there is an example later on). You should keep a careful record on each customer and debtor, as well as on the age of the debts.

6 Invoice at the earliest possible time, for example on despatch of the goods or on supply of the service, but for larger jobs try to get progress payments. For rush orders and special orders you should aim to get prepayment.

7 If you can get free issue materials, try to subcontract on that basis. If there are deliveries available to you with free credit, then take them if they are goods you know you will be able to sell.

8 Do not allow credit to others on small orders – depending on the scale of business done with that customer. The cost of giving and controlling it could wipe out the profit.

9 Run an accounts system which issues an automatic reminder, a final reminder, and 'last-resort' procedures, that is, debt-collecting agency/solicitor's letter. Try to find out who authorizes payment of your invoices in the other firm and aim to strike up a good relationship with them. You may be paid more quickly that way than if you keep writing nasty letters.

10 You must decide at what point you will stop supplying a customer who pays slowly.

11 Only offer settlement discounts if they are already built into your price. If they are, a generous discount for immediate payment may help trade to flow smoothly.

Terms of credit are very varied. In many industries they are recommended or set by trade associations; in others, they are recognized and accepted as custom of trade. You may well be able to extend your short-term funds by making fuller use of the trade credit offered by suppliers, and you should not let opportunities like this slip away.

Cash

Cash is a very precious asset and its ability to work is often ignored. It is part of the working capital fund and should be put to work all the time. Let us take a simple example which shows the power of money by measuring what it can do without any effort at all. If you deposit £20,000 in the money market at 10 per cent per annum, it will produce £2000 at the end of the twelve months, and you would not have to lift a finger to earn it. If you invest a similar amount in your business, it may produce the same amount of profit but you will have worked perhaps for ten hours each day, six days a week, and without holidays. With this in mind, it is important to make sure that while you work hard your money also works hard for you. Here are some points that may help:

1   If your business borrows money from a bank and you pay cash and cheques into the bank only once or twice each week, the business will suffer a substantial cost each day the cash and cheques are not deposited. The banks calculate overdraft interest on the amount borrowed each day, and any cash paid in would reduce the charges.

2   Cheques paid into your account do not give you instant cash. They originate from different banks and branches and they have to be sent back to them for clearance. Most cheques take at least three days to clear through the system, and much longer if a weekend or a Bank Holiday intervenes. This means that although you have paid the cheque into your account you cannot use the funds, even though your statement shows that the money was credited to your account on that day. Like everyone else you will have to wait until it is cleared through the banking system. If the amount of a cheque is all you have in your bank account and you draw the money before it is cleared, the bank will charge you interest on the amount you use. You need to bear this fact in mind – especially if you run a tightly controlled account – otherwise the bank charges will start to build up. You should always pay cheques into your bank on the day they are received for two reasons: first, so that they can be cleared quickly to give you the funds; second, in case they 'bounce', that is, they are not paid because the person giving you the cheque has insufficient funds. Any other system will cost you dearly.

3   There will be many times when your business has surplus funds – or money available for use temporarily. If you leave it in your current account in a bank, it will earn you practically nothing. The bank will give you a small benefit on funds left in your business current account known as 'abatement', which means that the money there will attract a low rate of interest, and it will be used only to reduce your bank charges on that account – but the interest will be very low. If you have funds

101

under £10,000, the best action to take is to open a deposit account. You can always transfer some or all of the deposit back to your current account very quickly, at the counter, or by telephone or letter. In the meantime, you will be earning a reasonable rate of interest on the funds. You may find that another financial institution will offer you a higher rate of interest and, as long as the funds do not have to be tied up for too long a period – some deposit schemes are set at six months or a year, or even longer – you should take the best rate.

If the sum exceeds £10,000, you should consider using the 'money market'. Your bank will 'place' the money for you in the inter-bank market – which is the banks' own market and is very safe – and you can choose how you want it to be placed: 'overnight', if you need it the next day; 'at call', so that you can ask for it whenever you like; 'without notice'; 'one day', 'two days', and so on – at any notice period up to five years. The rates of interest vary all the time but they are much higher than the banks' deposit accounts, and, once a rate has been agreed, it is fixed until the time arranged runs out. At the same time, many financial institutions offer competitive rates for deposits and, providing the period it has to remain with them is right for you, the funds may be placed there. But do not let the idea of high interest run away with you. If you place your money for a fixed term of say, three months in the money market or on deposit with a financial institution, and you decide after a while that you want to change your mind, you cannot have it back before that time limit expires. Three months definitely means three months! Nevertheless, by depositing surplus funds, you ensure that your money is working for you during the time you have it. Many businesses find that they receive a great deal of money which can be deposited, for example, travel agents take deposits, estate agents do the same, solicitors control clients' accounts, some builders or production companies take prepayments, and so on.

4 You should centralize all the cash accounts in your business. All too often the amounts held in various offices or working areas are forgotten. You will find them under the labels of postage tills, petty cash, floats and emergency accounts, and

by bringing all these sums of money together, the total amount held can be better controlled and greatly reduced.

5   For the developing business, it could pay to look at the computer services offered by the banks or by computer bureaux. Some of them may be able to help with your cash flow or secure other economies. For example, the payroll service could save four days on the wages bill because your bank account will only be debited on the day your employees' accounts are credited – no matter with which bank they may have their accounts. The direct debiting service can save two days at least, and there are many other services, such as purchase and sales ledgers, cheque reconciliation, computer to microfilm, and magnetic tape services.

Factoring may allow a reduction in staff and give you an improved cash flow, despite the fact that charges are made for the service. The factoring company takes over the sales ledger and looks after the bad debts for you. But you are still responsible if a customer does not pay. The factor pays about 80 per cent of each invoice to you but you no longer need staff to run the sales ledger or to chase customers for payment. If you sell goods to a large number of customers, this service could be very helpful to you.

You will see from this information that good use can be made of cash, although it has to be manipulated all the time. But these suggestions are not once-and-for-all measures, or jobs which need to be done once a year. You will have to examine your business all the time to find ways of cutting costs, using cash to its best advantage, and improving your cash flow.

Changes in borrowing

If you have financed your business by an overdraft, which has become impossible to repay by normal trading operations, you will be running at a high risk. An overdraft is repayable on demand – after reasonable notice is given (which is about one month) – and if this happened you could find yourself in serious financial difficulties. Before any problems arise you would be wise to go to your lender and renegotiate all your financial arrangements, either by getting a medium-term loan to cover your needs over a period of time, a long-term loan, some form of government aid, a sale-and-leaseback arrangement on your business premises, or a long-term insurance company mortgage.

Stock control

If you are in manufacturing, wholesale or the retail business, stock can tie up a large amount of your working capital. The importance of control to ensure profitability and liquidity cannot be overemphasized. It is an area which demands your personal supervision, regardless of whether you run a small or large business. Before we look at a control method, let us consider a number of conflicting factors which arise when deciding your stock levels.

- **Service to customers** You will wish to enjoy a reputation for efficient service, whether you are selling goods to wholesalers, retailers, or directly to the public. If you cannot meet customer demand at the right time, orders may be switched to your competitors, and you may never get them back.

- **Maintaining production targets** In a manufacturing business you must make certain that sufficient supplies of raw materials, components parts and partly finished goods are available to continue production smoothly.

- **Purchase of raw materials** You may be very smart to buy raw materials in bulk as a hedge against inflation, but if the situation is not controlled properly it could end in disaster. You will need to have a clear idea of future market demand, the costs involved and the effect that bulk buying will have on your cash flow – and you have to get it right!

- **Working capital** From the point of view of financial control, your aim should be to keep stocks at a minimum practical level. Stock needs to be converted into cash as soon as possible if your cash flow is to operate properly.

In a small business, complex stock control procedures are unnecessary if your thinking is clearly defined. The three most

104

important items to remember are:

1 **Re-order level** This is the level at which replacement stocks should be ordered. In arriving at this figure, make allowance for the delay before supplies are received, the stocks used during this period, and a safety margin.

2 **Re-order quantity** You should consider the costs to your business of holding stock, set against possible discounts for quantity.

3 **Checking deliveries** When deliveries are made to your premises, great care is needed to make sure that you receive every item that has been ordered. Many businesses lose money regularly because a clerk or some other employee does not check the deliveries. They sign the delivery form but there may be shortages which have to be written off when the inventory is done. This can become a regular feature with some delivery men, especially if they recognize an incompetent clerk, and it could prove to be very expensive for your business.

See Figure 3 for an example of a stock control form. The rate of stock turnover can be very revealing. A low rate suggests that you may need to tighten your control because stock is not being converted into profit fast enough. *A simple test is to divide annual sales less gross profit by average stock – this will show the number of times stock has turned over during the year.*

Figure 3   *Stock control form (use a separate page for each item)*

Item	Actual stock	Re-order level	Re-order quantity	Last order	
				Date	Amount

You will need to examine, modify and reduce the level of your stock regularly. Slow moving lines should be removed and you should check whether the business is run by the 80/20 rule – where 20 per cent of the range accounts for 80 per cent of the value. If so, there is a need to question why you are holding the other 80 per cent which accounts for only 20 per cent of the value. It is advisable to operate stock control and re-ordering systems so that you can eliminate stock without running the risk of shortages. A continuous inventory-taking system is preferred to the traditional annual stock-taking with its high overtime costs, and it may be that you can do this on your own (or share someone else's) computer. You will need to look at average age comparisons of items in the stock range in order to find out if the 80/20 rule is operating. Stock room security is vital, as pilferage has often played havoc in many good businesses. But, above all, you should remember that the cost of holding stock includes the cost of the finance it represents, the cost of delivery, of obsolescence (dead stock), depreciation, warehousing, handling, protection and insurance. With these factors in mind, you should place your stock under close scrutiny and control, and take every step to reduce it to a minimum level and keep it moving.

Debtor/creditor control

Debtor control
Efficient control of debtors is a major part of sound financial management, yet it is often done haphazardly. Payment by debtors for goods and services received is a major source of cash for your business, and all you need is a simple control system to make sure that a proper cash flow is maintained. A regular check is extremely important to avoid the danger of overdue accounts becoming bad debts. The effect of bad debts on profitability is not always appreciated. For example, if your business earns a net profit of 10 per cent, a bad debt of £1000 will cancel the profit on £10,000 of sales. Not a very bright prospect!

The production of a monthly debtor analysis (see Figure 4) is the easiest method of noting your debtor position at a glance. The information you need can be taken from either your record of unpaid invoices or from your ledger. This will allow you to examine the age of debts, especially those overdue for payment.

Figure 4 *Debtor analysis form as at 30 June (use a separate page for each customer and update at the end of each month)*

Customer	Amount of debt			Total	Remarks
	1 month	2 months	3 months and over		
Totals					

Unless you are certain of your customers' financial standing, you should always check them out before delivering the first order. This can be done by getting a reference through your bank, or by approaching a credit agency or a trade protection society. You should check the creditworthiness of your customers regularly, especially if you supply a large proportion of your goods or services to one firm. You should keep well in mind that if they suffer financial difficulties it could also affect you and cause serious damage to your cash flow. Allocate a credit limit to each customer and keep checking that the amount owed is within the agreed figure. In the case of a new customer, you may not wish to supply further goods until previous deliveries have been paid for, and you will not want to extend credit until a good relationship has been established.

An efficient invoicing and debt collection system is a vital part of debtor control. Some practical hints are as follows:

1   Ensure that invoices are sent out at the time goods are despatched.

2   Refer to your debtor analysis for overdue items and send a statement or letter.

3   If no response is received, you may have to telephone or visit your customer to find out the reason for non-payment. Beware of lame excuses used to delay and try to establish a firm date for payment.

4   If your customer still does not pay, you may have to go to your solicitor or to a debt collection agency.

5   If your customer has a temporary cash flow problem you may decide to extend credit. This is a matter of judgement and it may be advisable to stop further deliveries until the situation becomes clear.

6   Make sure that you always collect payments when they are due. You will gain respect from your customers if you show that you maintain efficient control.

Credit control

Receipt of payments from debtors has a major influence on your cash flow but payments due to creditors are equally important. It is all too easy to make prompt payment of small amounts leaving larger invoices until later, only to find that you do not have enough money to pay them. The result could be the start of legal proceedings by a creditor, if you cannot resolve the problem quickly. A reputation for slow payment can also lead to suppliers demanding cash for goods, under-delivering, or not delivering at all. Therefore, while you are able to obtain credit, amounts owed should be strictly controlled. An analysis of creditors can help you in this matter. See Figure 5.

Expenses

Expenses charged by salesmen and executives should be controlled very tightly. If you run the business by yourself – with just a few staff for support – you may enjoy the luxury of charging everything to the business, but make sure that it does not get out of hand. The zest for the good life may be very enjoyable, but the extent of fringe benefits is unlimited, and can act as a drag on the business. Many good companies have foundered because the

Figure 5 *Creditor analysis form as at 30 June (use a separate form for each creditor and update at the end of each month)*

Customer	Amount of debt			Total	Remarks
	1 month	2 months	3 months and over		
Totals					

executives purchased expensive new cars, enjoyed regular expensive lunches and dinners daily, inviting their husbands or wives at weekends, and arranged for a multitude of extras for personal use, ranging from home computers to hi-fi equipment – all charged to the accounts of the business. Some businesses have succeeded despite such indulgences, but the strain has been enormous. It is advisable to live in moderation until success arrives, and part of the plan is to reduce unnecessary expenditure to the lowest possible level.

Some salesmen tend to be extravagant and, caught up in the excitement of getting an order, may feel that almost any expense is justified. If the trouble is taken to explain to them how large a proportion of their sales revenue is lost through their expenses, you are more likely to get their co-operation. With their help, you might be able to devise an incentive scheme which concentrates more on profitability, and, if cash flow is a concern, the same scheme could point out the disadvantages of credit sales.

The question of expenses also includes costs relating to postage, telephone calls and petrol paid for by the business. You must keep strict control over these items. The cost of postage will be very high if staff use franking machines or postage stamps for their own use. Tales of horror have included the clerk who brought in packages daily to pioneer his own private business so that all the postal charges were paid for by his employer – this went on for nearly two years. There was also the case of an assistant who operated a direct mail service for her brother in the same way for nearly a year.

A horticultural business in Somerset found that it had difficulty maintaining its profits and the blame was placed firmly on costs, inflation and the narrowness of margins as a result of severe competition. A consultant friend of the owner was asked to analyse the problem more specifically so that progress could be made in future years.

He started with internal overheads and suggested that one of the three office staff should be released. There was only sufficient work for two but the three women employed had adjusted their schedules to fit the three of them. There were five telephones in the office and three should be terminated as two office staff could not answer more than two telephones. The heating system was always on at too high a level and even in mid winter the windows of the office had to be opened for periods each day. Lights were sometimes left on at night and electric kettles without cut-out switches were left boiling if both staff members were occupied. The senior woman was allowed to charge the price of a newspaper each day to the company, as well as magazines (a perk from past days), and was awarded half her home telephone rental (a relic of a time when emergencies occurred). She also charged petrol for coming to and from work and for unwarranted miscellaneous journeys. Postal costs were high due to the despatch of brochures at different times during the year but there was no post book kept for record purposes.

Externally, two salesmen ran riot with the cost of petrol, often travelling for long distances for personal reasons at weekends and charging it to the business expense account. Ancillary expenses for food, drink, parking charges and van repairs were extremely high and often nothing to do with the business itself. The owner accepted the final recommendations and, while losing one member of staff, ignored the grumblings of the other staff. The result was that the business ran more efficiently and saved over £10,000 in costs in the first year.

Telephone charges may reach frightening proportions if there is no control. There are three serious types of wastage: firstly, staff will use the telephone for personal calls at both peak and non-peak times which are paid for by your business; secondly, while they are making personal telephone calls they are not working for you; thirdly, while they are using the telephone, business cannot be received from customers – the staff are blocking the lines. One small company reduced its system from ten telephones to four, and its telephone bill dropped to one-eighth. There are thousands of similar stories which can be told. In addition, money can be saved by telephoning during the less expensive afternoon period whenever possible.

Control of petrol is more difficult because it means that every journey has to be measured carefully, but it is more important that you should decide whether the journey is necessary. Weekend joy-rides by salesmen in company cars may be part of the perks, but they should be prepared to pay for the petrol themselves. The calculation is very simple – for every thirty miles you eliminate, you save the price of one gallon of petrol!

Additional expenses relate to pilferage by customers, employees and outsiders. Customer theft can amount to between 2 to 3 per cent of stock, while employee theft is unlimited. It may begin with borrowing a ballpoint pen and extend to much larger items. Businesses without security checks also suffer from outsider theft. Micro computers, typewriters and even filing cabinets have disappeared from business premises when 'the boss' is out to lunch – by 'a man' who said he had come to take the equipment away for repair. It proves that you cannot be too careful!

Cutting labour costs

The cost of labour can form a large part of the expenditure in your business, and during growth it can increase in leaps and bounds. The biggest stumbling block in cutting labour costs, or holding down the rate of increase, is often poor planning. You may be able to control the situation in the following ways:

1 When you plan growth you need to justify every additional
   person, working out the effect they will have on producing
   extra earnings or meeting targets.

2 Skilled people must be used efficiently. You should find out
   whether a larger proportion of their work could be done by less
   skilled people. In other words, many skilled workers spend a
   great deal of time on routine tasks that could be done by
   lower-paid workers.

3 Overrtime can be very expensive. If it becomes a regular
   feature, personnel come to regard it as part of their routine and
   their wages. When this happens it becomes difficult to get
   them back to normal hours without offering them concessions.
   You should study patterns of overtime and of routine work. If
   they are regular and predictable, consider other ways of
   handling overloads. Subcontracting may be cheaper and more
   convenient, and for light work you may use outworkers. There
   are many keen, qualified, capable men and women unable to
   take on full-time jobs, who would be delighted to have regular
   part-time work.

4 The workload ought to be spread evenly over the year.
   Unavoidable peaks and troughs can sometimes be timed to
   coincide with fluctuations in the local workforce, which means
   that your business need not be overstaffed for part of the year.
   You must consider whether a peak in one section of the
   business could be timed to coincide with a trough in another,
   so that transfers of staff can be made at the right times.
   This would give workers a wider interest and help to develop
   their skills.

A business cannot expect to be self-sufficient, especially when
growth takes place, because growth causes work overload and the
need for new expertise. When this happens, contracting out can
be a useful way of helping your cash flow. For instance, if you
exceed the capacity of your distribution system, you could place a
particular region in the hands of an outside distributor or a
delivery contractor and save a great deal of capital expenditure. It
might be worth contracting out the whole packaging/distribution
function, saving you the cost of a new warehouse, more vans or

lorries, and more staff in the future. But do keep direct control of everything in which you and your company are really expert. For the rest, when facing a problem of organization, making a decision, work overload or recruitment, do not forget to consider using outside services.

A national tyre and exhaust replacement company which once had 110 administrative staff to run 90 depots, now runs 260 outlets for motorists with an administrative staff of 28, and will only need a few more when the target of 400 outlets is reached. Invoices, quotations, stock control, the payroll, marketing and promotions, management performance reports, local pricing policies, and even reports on workplace accidents are handled on a £2 million computer system.

The company insisted that it wanted its own fully custom-made computer system – not an adaptation of an existing system which would suit the company with a 'bit of adjustment'. The aim was month-end accounting within forty-eight hours, and one clerk and one manager per administrative function. The head office and administration have become merely support staff. Under the present system, a depot terminal gives a customer a quote on tyres, batteries, shock absorbers or exhaust systems. A sale is punched out on his terminal and the only printed copy is given to the customer with his guarantee. The day's stocktaking and administration, including reports on staff absences, take a mere ten minutes at the end of the day. During the night the office computer automatically dials each depot to note the daily takings, and the number of parts sold. The company attempts to have replacements for the depot's bin of some 1800 parts delivered within forty-eight hours.

Through a private viewdata system connected to the central computer system, regional managers can examine depots in terms of their sales performance. They can note, for example, if a manager is selling a high enough proportion of wheel balancing with tyre changes, and whether battery sales targets are being met. Where targets are not being met, action can be taken.

Suppliers, too, are linked to the system. A computer link is essential where there are substantial contracts with companies supplying parts. The system allows the company to analyse local sales patterns to determine the appropriate level of local stocks.

A regional manager can report a local competitor with a special offer and the system will see if the company can match, or better, the offer, and determine what price rises in other areas will be needed to compensate for the special discount.

The contingency plan

The measures set out above should help your business to remain liquid in normal times. But when the going gets rough, survival becomes important. You will have to find new sources of income, reduce expenditure quickly, and run a severe crash sales programme to reduce stocks as fast as possible. Equipment that is not used must be sold, as well as property, patents and anything else of value. Trade and other investments not useful to the immediate and urgent needs of the business must go. Harsh collection programmes for debtors will have to be arranged – it is no use worrying about goodwill when serious problems arise. Staff not working to capacity should be released; unsold equipment may be hired out to other businesses; and surplus accommodation should be let.

The contingency plan is not squeamish about cutting out waste, and it looks at everything that can be turned into cash or eliminated from expenses. At the end, you should consolidate what is left and carry out a complete re-organization of the business in its new state. In this way, impending disaster may be avoided and you may be able to turn your business into a smaller but very much more effective operation. However, one thing is certain, if you are a good manager you will review the business all the time, rather than wait until an emergency arrives.

Action Guidelines

1   Identify your working capital over the next year.

	1st qtr	2nd qtr	3rd qtr	4th qtr
Stock				
plus debtors				
minus creditors	_____	_____	_____	_____
equals working capital	_____	_____	_____	_____

2   How much cash are you paying next year for plant, equipment, stock? Can you help your cash flow by hire purchase, leasing or a stocking loan paid over a period of time?

3   Are you able to leave more money in the business yourself?

4   What trade credit are you getting from small, medium and large suppliers? Can you improve on the situation?

5   Have you checked whether you can get free issue materials, prepayments, free credit? Check with your industry or trade association.

6   Are you depositing spare cash? How much interest are you getting? Compare it with the money market and other institutions.

7   Can the computer services of the banks or computer bureaux help your business? Find out more about them.

115

8   Are your finances getting in a tangle? Should you renegotiate
your borrowing?

_____

_____

9   Are you controlling your stock as outlined? What is the number of
times your stock turns over during the year?

_____

_____

10   Do you operate on the 80/20 rule?

_____

_____

11   Complete a debtor and creditor analysis.

_____

_____

12   List all the expenses charged to the business last year and the
current year and check which items could have been avoided.

_____

_____

13   Have another look at your staff. Could you improve the situation?
Is it worth contracting work out?

_____

_____

14   Draw-up an emergency plan. What might you jettison or change? Can
you do it now – before the emergency arises?

_____

_____

_____

_____

_____

_____

_____

_____

6

What Kind of Money is Available from Your Bank and Other Sources

- Do you have to go to a bank for money?
- How do you assess your needs?
- What is the right kind of borrowing?
- Are there special schemes that would help your business?
- How do you know whether you need short, medium or long-term finance?
- Can you borrow for ten years and not repay until that time is up?
- Are you out of your league with equity finance?

Assessing your needs

You will probably have started your business with some of your own money, perhaps with the help of your family, friends and with a bank overdraft. You may have started up your own business from scratch or bought an existing business. If the business was already there you will have wanted finance for expansion. As well as money for new buildings, plant and machinery, this includes working capital for building up stocks, for work-in-progress and for more trade debtors. There are a number of different kinds of finance for each business need, most of them involving borrowing and repayment, but you will still own 100 per cent of your business. In other cases, where the

117

balance sheet becomes unstructured, you may decide that to grow larger and faster it could be worth your while to give up some of the equity – to allow others to take a share in the business. But we shall come to that later on.

Whichever way you started, as you become successful and grow you will find that profits ploughed back into the business are not enough to keep it going. If that happens, it does not mean that you are becoming inefficient or that there is something wrong – growth uses up more money. Obviously, you cannot keep going back to your bank for a larger overdraft every time you need more cash, and it is at this stage that you need to realize that there are certain methods of finance which are geared to different needs. So you have to find out why you want more money and then choose the kind of finance that will suit your business. If you do not, your business will always be hungry for cash and you will spend more time worrying about money than concentrating on sales and customers.

Banks and institutional lenders have tailored their schemes to fit nearly all business situations, so you will not have too much trouble. Different situations require different solutions. For example, it would be foolish to borrow on overdraft to buy freehold buildings rather than to get a mortgage. The property would not be producing earnings, yet your overdraft is charged on a daily basis. A mortgage is a perfect answer to this problem. So you need to choose the right sort of finance for your business operations very carefully. But before you try to work it out for yourself, let us look at the opportunities one by one, so that you understand what is being offered.

The problem of working out your best means of finance may be very difficult for you to solve. If that is the case, you ought to find a good financial adviser. Such a person may be your local bank manager, a specialist banker, your accountant, the Small Firms Service officer, or some other expert. If you do get an adviser, you are not committed in any way. For example, information given by your bank manager does not commit you to have to take finance from the bank. It is only advice and you should not feel obliged to take it up. However, if you do ask for advice, you will need to keep your adviser fully informed of your business development and plans – otherwise the whole thing is pointless – and the adviser, in turn, will need to make regular visits to see your business at first hand. Bank

118

managers are usually helpful, but there are many of them who have never visited the premises of some of their customers, and they try to solve many matters by calling you in, or by telephone. If that is happening to you, the bank manager may not be giving you his best attention. Another point to remember is that an independent adviser may be able to arrange introductions to institutional lenders, and they can help you to prepare and present applications which have a first-class chance of success.

In most cases, you will probably go to your bank manager for advice because the bank can offer you a wide range of financial service. But there are other methods of finance – some far better and cheaper than bank loans – especially from the government, the EEC, and other institutions. So before you go to the bank, review the situation and work out the forms of finance which will best suit your business. If you decide that no other source can offer you better services and advice than your bank, then so be it! But if you come to that conclusion after you have read this book, you have skipped the best parts! So let us start at the beginning.

In assessing your financial needs, it is important that account is taken not only of your balance sheet and future profits, but also of cash flow. It is no use claiming that you are making fantastic profits if there is no cash to pay the wages. The cash available to a business is what it has in its bank balance and any other deposits – but not the amount owed by debtors – together with any lines of credit which have not been used up. Finance for expansion is best planned well in advance. It should be based on forecasts of sales, costs, investment expenditure and profits which can be ploughed back, but it can be risky to place too much reliance on funds earned in your business to meet planned expenditure. Profit forecasts are by their nature very uncertain, and if they fall short you could be forced to borrow at very short notice, perhaps at a time when the government is operating a credit squeeze and lending is being restricted. For these reasons, you should try to keep a cushion of finance, agreed by a bank or an institution, which is not being used; and you would be well advised always to know where next to turn to for extra finance, rather than wait until an emergency arrives and rush round in a panic, unprepared. You need to keep a tight control over money matters.

There are many sources of finance available and the danger is that you might make use of too many of them at the same time. A number of difficulties will arise if you borrow from many different lenders, mainly because every loan demands separate repayment each month or quarter. You will be paying out too much money – far more than your business can stand, unless it is earning very large profits. Also, if you spread yourself too thinly amongst a lot of lenders, each one of them will regard you as a tiny customer rather than a fair-sized business. You should look for finance from a small number of lenders, and make sure that each of them is fully informed of the facilities granted to you by the others. This is the only way to allow your business to develop soundly. Honesty is the best policy with financiers – and do not forget it! If a lender comes to hear that you have not disclosed information that he ought to know, you may have closed that source of credit for ever.

The right kind of borrowing

When starting from scratch, some loan finance may be needed which is secured against the assets of the new business. You may retain full ownership by raising the money within your circle of family, friends or business associates. More often, the local bank manager is asked to help. The banks provide overdrafts to help finance working capital and trade, and they can provide small, medium and long-term loans – in proportion to the balance sheet – to be secured against the business assets the loan purchases or against your personal assets. Banks also have corporate finance divisions, merchant banking arms, development capital offshoots, and equity companies. Your bank manager can put you in touch with any one of these, and perhaps offer other sources of capital. Banks can lend at long-term, but they are more willing to provide short or medium-term working capital, and they may be reluctant to lend where there is high risk, even if you offer security of property and other fixed assets. Just because you can supply a lot of security it does not mean that it will turn a bad business proposition into a good one! The bank will want to see evidence that you are prepared to risk your own money, either by injecting funds as share capital or by putting up personal property as security. They dislike foreclosing when businesses go wrong, so even when a loan is fully secured a bank manager will still wish to be assured that the business is doing well, and to be kept fully informed on its progress and prospects.

Before running the gauntlet of lending facilities, let us stop for a moment to ask some simple questions about borrowing from a bank in a question and answer form:

Q How much do you need to borrow?

A After you have worked out the amount – taking into account every kind of expenditure – add 10 per cent for contingency purposes.

Q Should you approach a bank first, before working out the details?

A Definitely. The bank manager will help you with a great deal of advice. It is far better to do this than to complete your application and find out that you have missed out some important elements.

Q What kinds of financial packages will suit your company best?

A Your bank manager will arrange an interview with financial experts to assist you. The interview may cost a small fee but it will be worth it in the long run.

Q What will your bank allow you to borrow?

A A business can only ask for facilities within its own financial boundaries. A small business could not hope to borrow a million pounds, but there is no specific limit – unless government restrictions prevail in times of credit squeezes.

Q Do the banks have sufficient resources?

A Yes – except when government restrictions prevail – there are ample funds at all times for the banks to lend.

Q What happens if your bank turns you down?

A Go to another bank, or a financial institution. But check your application. The fault may lie in a poor presentation, misinterpretation, or insufficient information. If you are turned down more than twice you need to re-examine the situation carefully.

Q Do bank managers treat all applications fairly, or does prejudice creep in?

A It is wise to have a good relationship with your bank manager. If not, change your branch, or change your bank. Naturally, a

good business will merit good treatment. However, one which is often forced to go into the red, or which is constantly borrowing to survive, could become a high-grade risk.
Therefore, it is not a matter of prejudice but assessing the risk according to the business application.

The periods for which money is needed can be short, medium and long-term, and on a permanent basis, and the main kinds of financing are as follows:

1 Short-term finance is used to finance:
    Seasonal fluctuation
    General working capital needs
    Bridging finance before making a more permanent arrangement
    Minor fixed assets with a short working life.

2 Medium-term finance (three to ten years) is used to finance:
    Fixed asset purchase (major ones if the cash flow is very strong)
    Funding the hard core element of overdrafts
    Increased working capital requirements
    Small-scale business takeovers

3 Long-term finance (ten to twenty years) is used to finance:
    Major fixed asset purchases with a long life
    Permanent working capital
    Corporate takeovers

4 Permanent finance is mainly used for:
    Broadening the borrowing platform
    Financing major fixed asset acquisitions with a long life
    Financing corporate takeovers.

Short-term finance

Overdrafts
Bank facilities usually take the form of an agreed overdraft and, because the bank handles your income from all sources, the balance on which the interest is charged fluctuates day by day. Overdrafts are legally repayable on demand, but a bank cannot do so without giving reasonable notice – which could be as short as

122

one month. Usually, you will be told that you can rely on the facility for a year, six months, or for a shorter term.

Bank overdrafts are the most widely used kind of short-term finance. Their advantages to a business include the following:

- The system is simple and arrangements can be set up quickly.
- The system is flexible. Sums can be drawn or repaid within the agreed limit at any time entirely at your option and without prior notice.
- It is one of the cheaper forms of borrowing. Interest is payable only on the amount outstanding each day. Charges are made at the end of the quarter or half-year.
- Once agreed, an overdraft facility is generally renewable, subject to the creditworthiness of your business. If things are not going well for you, the bank may withdraw it.

The main disadvantages are that an overdraft is subject to renewal every year; it is repayable on demand; and the rate of interest is increased immediately if the bank's base rate is raised.

The banks will not normally interfere with your business when an overdraft is granted, but they will expect you to keep them fully informed of your financial position, not only by presenting them with your annual accounts but also through periodic statements of debtors' and creditors' balances, stock estimates and orders in hand.

When overdrafts are used to buy fixed assets, the bank will generally want a fixed charge or mortgage on the assets concerned. But in the case of overdrafts for working capital requirements they often make large advances without security if they are satisfied that the business is sound. When this is in doubt, although the net asset position may still show a high degree of solvency, the bank may, at any time, ask for a fixed charge or mortgage on the fixed assets with a floating charge on the current assets. Where the financial position is less secure, they may ask for guarantees.

Bill finance
A bill of exchange is similar to a post-dated cheque which can be

123

sold for cash at a discount. If you sell goods to another business, you will be able to get cash for them shortly after they are despatched, while allowing the buyer to defer payment until they arrive or until there has been time to market them.

Trade bills   A *trade bill* is drawn by the person selling the goods and accepted by the buyer, and it is payable on a set date. It can be offered for discount to either a discount house or to your own bank. The rate of discount charged depends on the credit standing of the traders and sometimes on the goods concerned. There are two things to consider with this form of finance: firstly, if you pay accounts by cheque on a due or perhaps overdue date, there may be objections to accepting a bill which will be presented for payment at a definite date. Secondly, to discount the bill through a bank or discount house involves taking bankers' references to examine the creditworthiness of both drawer and acceptor. The drawer becomes liable for the proceeds of the bill after discounting in the event of default by the acceptor.

The system sounds complicated but it is not so in practice; you simply arrange for the bills to be discounted and your accountant will advise you how to draw them.

Acceptance credits   Provided that there is a sale of goods, you can draw a bill on a merchant bank or accepting house. The bill is known as a prime bank bill and can be discounted at a very good rate. Normally, a manufacturer or merchant needing finance to buy goods goes to an accepting house, which is a merchant bank specializing in acceptance credits. If the bank is agreeable, it issues a letter of credit to you for an agreed amount, and for either a fixed or indefinite period. This letter of credit permits you to draw bills on the accepting house, which by accepting them assumes responsibility for their payment at maturity. The bills are usually drawn at three months' sight and must involve a commercial transaction, such as the purchase of raw materials or the sale of finished goods. The bills, after acceptance, are sold to one of the London discount houses, the proceeds being paid to you on that day. Therefore, you obtain cash immediately. If at the date that the bills mature you still wish to use the facilities, arrangements can be made for the credit to be continued. The cost of finance by the bank bill may be cheaper than borrowing by overdraft or fixed loan, but this will depend on monetary conditions at the time.

The advantages of bills are that:

- The cost of bill finance is usually competitive with bank overdrafts, and may be cheaper.
- If bills are sold to a bank or discount house you can calculate the cost of financing the transaction, because the rate of discount is fixed and not affected by any changes in interest rates.
- You can shift part of your financing from overdraft to bill finance. Overdraft facilities may then be released for other purposes.
- Bill finance may be useful when conditions for obtaining longer-term funds tend to be difficult, because of high interest rates or a shortage of funds for long-term investment. But bills should not be relied on too heavily for longer-term needs.

Hire-purchase

Hire-purchase is a source of short to medium-term credit for the use of capital equipment over an agreed hire period. At the end of this, the legal title passes to you on the exercise of an option to buy the equipment for a small sum of money. The fact that the agreement has a fixed period for repayment means that the balance cannot be called in on demand, and so you can complete your planning and budgeting with confidence. After payment of an agreed deposit, the equipment will be invoiced by the supplier to the finance house which then becomes the legal owner. It is then hired to you under agreement, but you are not the owner until you make the final option payment.

To be suitable for hire-purchase the machinery or goods should ideally:

- Be capable of easy identification (that is, not components of a larger item of plant, or unidentifiable stocks of spare parts).
- Have a life expectancy greater than the period of the hire-purchase agreement, and they should have a market value

greater than the amount owed under the agreement.

- Enjoy a high earnings potential so that they can earn sufficient to pay off the indebtedness over the period of the agreement.

Repayment terms are normally from two to five years, unless the goods are specifically controlled by a government order requiring a shorter period. If you decide to complete the transaction and buy the assets earlier than the termination date of the agreement, this can generally be arranged. The hire-purchase company will accept a lump sum in lieu of the rentals remaining to be paid, usually with a discount on the interest charge.

Factoring

Factoring is the provision of a sales ledger accounting service with credit insurance and with, if required, the provision of finance against the security of outstanding debtors. Usually, the factor takes over the sales ledger and pays some 80 per cent of invoice values to the manufacturer, and chases bad debts. But there are different forms of factoring and you should check which service you need with the factor.

The types of problems which may be resolved by a factor are:

- A cash flow created through expansion.
- Large amounts of capital tied up in the debtors' ledgers.
- A need for protection against bad debts.
- Overspending in non-productive areas such as sales-ledger accounting, debt collecting, and credit information.
- Difficulty in handling overseas business effectively.
- Worries about credit control.

The advantages of factoring are:

- It provides a complete sales ledger and accounting service.
- It protects against bad debts.
- It is a quicker method of settling debts.

- It offers expert guidance on credit control.
- It is an opportunity to obtain prepayment of up to 80 per cent of approved debts.
- It controls cash flow.
- It allows advantage to be taken of suppliers' discounts.
- It provides an up-to-the-minute sales analysis if required.
- It enhances credit status because the factor becomes the company's only debtor.
- It helps in overseas markets through export factoring.

The savings may be considerable and include costs of expensive executive time, postage, stationery, telephone bills, legal fees, salaries of sales-ledger staff, and the cost of space and machinery for accounting. Factoring eliminates bad debts and the costs of credit investigations.

A company in Newcastle employing thirty people manufactured engineering parts which it supplied to a large number of small firms in the UK. Each month it would issue invoices to customers and, with them, the staff of three women sent out the usual reminders to late payers. A small element of bad debts was a problem and the company used a credit agency to try to recover them. The main problem was that the company was expanding as demand increased but the overdraft at the bank was limited in size. This meant that the cash flow became restricted. The bank agreed to increase the overdraft limit to the company but, clearly, this would be only a temporary relief. At the same time, the bank manager was concerned that the company might be overtrading. One of the directors noticed that the bank had a factoring subsidiary. He approached the bank manager and explained that his company issued invoices regularly to many different customers and would seem to comply with factoring criteria. After a meeting, the factors agreed to take over the sales ledger of the company and place all the accounts on its computer. They paid the company 80 per cent of every invoice issued, undertook all the mailing, and made arrangements to collect bad debts. The company was required to pay interest on the advances and a small percentage fee for the service. On the other hand, it retained its overdraft for further expansion, reduced its office staff by one person, and discontinued its arrangement with the credit agency concerning bad debts. Hence, the cost of saving on one staff member, telephone calls, stationery, etc. was sufficient alone to pay for the percentage fee to the factoring company, without having any attendant problems.

A potential factoring client is likely to be as follows:

- Incorporated under the UK Companies Act.
- Has an annual turnover of £100,000 or more.
- Established long enough to have at least one, preferably two, sets of audited accounts available showing a reasonable profit record.
- Does not sell direct to the public.
- Not engaged in long-term contracts involving progress payments.
- Not selling complex, expensive capital equipment.

These requirements are not hard-and-fast rules and you should contact a factor if you think you might qualify.

Invoice discounting
This is a means of generating cash by selling to a factoring company or a finance house, at a discount, either a selection of invoices on a firm's larger debtors or the entire sales ledger. Your business may reach the point where, even with the help of bank finance, expansion is being affected through the amount of working capital tied up in book debts. Where the credit extended to customers is fairly short, say thirty or sixty days, it may be possible to convert a proportion of book debts into cash by discounting invoices to meet this need for short-term revolving finance.

An agreement is made with the factor/finance house to discount, and you 'offer' invoices to them, guaranteeing payment of any debts they may purchase. If the 'offer' is accepted, you will be sent payment of up to 80 per cent of the total amount. The system differs from factoring in that you are responsible for the collection of debts sold. The cost of the service depends upon the risks and administrative costs involved; it includes an interest charge on the amount advanced plus a service charge. A potential borrower offering a book debt as security will find that lender will be more willing to make the advance if the debt is insured, that is, the client pays a premium to an insurance company in return for the amount of the invoice if the debt is not recovered. The cost of the insurance will depend on the amounts involved and the risks attached to the debt.

Invoice discounting is a simple, flexible source of finance enabling a business temporarily to increase its working capital while maintaining a normal relationship with customers, who need not know of the arrangement. As it can affect the value of a lending bank's security, however, your bank should be informed if you intend to raise finance in this way.

Leasing
Leasing is a form of finance by which a leasing company buys plant or equipment required and chosen by you, and leases it to you at an agreed rental. A leasing arrangement is essentially a contract whereby the leasing organization retains ownership of the leased equipment, while you have possession and use it, with payment of agreed rentals over a specified period.

The advantages of leasing are as follows:

- It enables you to profit by using both equipment and capital, without tying up working funds – allowing them to find other profitable employment.

- A capital investment programme normally creates increased demands on working capital to finance stocks and work-in-progress; leasing helps to preserve bank and other sources of credit for operating needs.

- Owning old equipment can prove costly. Leasing can make the acquisition of expensive new machinery financially painless.

- Since the user never acquires title to the equipment, no entry is required in the balance sheet, allowing the presentation of 'clean' financial statements and preserving important balance sheet ratios.

- The flexibility of leasing, and the many combinations of

payment terms available, allow wide scope in drafting a lease which fits the cash flow circumstances of a lessee, and gives you greater freedom in investment decisions.

- The ability to obtain the use of new equipment for a small rental is an important aid to budgeting.
- Leasing offers a practical alternative to equity financing and prevents broadening the ownership of your business.
- It combats the cost and effects of inflation.
- Leasing ensures fixed costs for a known period.

Provided you fulfil your side of the contract, the leasing company cannot make changes in agreed arrangements. Hence, leasing rentals cannot be increased (unless the terms specifically allow for this), nor can the lease be withdrawn in the event of a change in economic conditions or a credit squeeze.

Block discounting

This is a useful means of finance for retailers who sell goods by hire-purchase or credit sales, or who rent out goods to customers. It is particularly suitable to creditworthy dealers in small-unit consumer durables, such as stereo equipment, washing machines, refrigerators, televisions, cameras, etc.

Finance is forwarded to you by finance houses on the agreements while you continue to collect repayments from the customer on their behalf. The amount discounted may be about 65 per cent of the gross rental income over a period – say, three years for television rentals.

In most cases, however, rather than carrying out detailed calculations for each agreement discounted, an initial payment of between £150 and £170 may be paid for each agreement in the case of television rentals. The amount will be fixed for a particular dealer and will depend on his standing, the amount of discounting done with the finance institution, and the average nominal cost price of the sets rented out.

The advantages of block discounting are:

- It releases capital invested in rental stock or instalment credit finance for business use elsewhere.
- It enables you to increase turnover and profitability by using the released capital.
- It allows you to take full advantage of trade discounts by paying promptly.
- It offers a reliable confidential credit source in addition to banking arrangements.
- It enables you to offer flexible terms to selective customers to match competitors' activities.
- It retains the agreements in your name, preserving the goodwill and business potential generated by personal service.

A business in East Anglia operated three consumer durable goods shops – mainly selling stereo equipment, televisions, washing machines and refrigerators. During an extended consumer boom it increased its sales substantially. It could cope adequately with an expanding turnover in direct sales but there were problems coping with the television rental side. The long-term potential of rentals had been recognized some years earlier but, the high demand for customer service meant that part of the business had had to expand faster than anticipated. The main problem was that the retailer had to bear all the initial costs of rental. For a payment of one month's fee by a customer, the wholesale cost of the television set had to be paid to the manufacturer, a service function and a workshop had to be maintained, vans were required, petrol had to be purchased, etc., etc. The early outcome was a drain on the cash flow. It was then that the owner discovered that a finance house operated block discounting and he arranged to meet them in order to discuss the matter. In due course, they agreed to the following:

1 The retailer would continue to collect rental payments from customers.
   All new rental agreements would be passed to the finance house for which 65 per cent of the gross rental income would be paid to the retailer.
3 Rental agreements in existence would be considered and the better quality rentals would qualify for similar advances.

4 The finance house would charge interest on the amount advanced.
5 The retailer would be responsible for bad debts.

This arrangement took much of the financial strain off the business which utilized this credit source in addition to banking arrangements.

Stocking finance
Stocking finance is a useful means of assistance provided for motor vehicle or caravan dealers, or to retailers in appliances and consumer durables.

Dealers' requirements are:

- Sufficient stock-in-trade for resale to offer immediate delivery, without tying up capital, that is, demonstration merchandise without immediate capital expenditure.
- The stock has to be self-liquidating, selling fairly quickly and reducing the loan which is 'topped' up when you buy new stock.
- To be able to rebuild stock continuously and freedom to sell the merchandise at the most advantageous time.
- A regular predictable cash outflow to assist budgeting.
- Tax relief on interest paid.

The advantages are:

- You have a revolving loan up to an agreed limit, usually secured.
- The capital is repaid as and when the stock is sold.
- Further advances are available up to the credit limit on demand.
- Interest payments are made monthly or quarterly depending on the requirements.
- Interest is charged on the daily balance outstanding at a rate linked to a base rate. The rate will vary with the amount of retail business.

- There is immediate use of the merchandise.
- The title passes to the dealer on termination of the finance agreement.
- The agreement may be settled at any time prior to the scheduled completion date, with a rebate of charges for early settlement.
- Finance is for a fixed term which cannot be recalled or reduced on demand like an overdraft.

Where to get short-term finance

The banks are the main providers of overdrafts and short-term loans. There is generally no minimum amount set for these facilities. The banks also provide trade bill and acceptance credit services and, through their specialist subsidiary and associate companies, leasing, instalment credit, and factoring facilities.

Merchant banks such as the accepting houses provide short-term loans, discounts of trade bills, and acceptance credits. Many of them are also able to supply specialist facilities such as leasing, but they are chiefly interested in propositions involving sums of £50,000 and more.

Other British and foreign banks provide short-term facilities including overdrafts and loans. They are generally interested in situations likely to involve international trade, and, in the case of foreign banks, trading links with their countries of origin. Some have subsidiaries and associate companies specializing in leasing and instalment credit.

Finance houses provide instalment credit, both hire-purchase and credit sales; they also supply leasing and block discount facilities. Many of them are part of larger financial institutions, especially banks.

Discount houses discount bank bills and trade bills for companies engaged in domestic and overseas trade.

Factoring companies provide factoring/invoice discounting services. The larger ones are mostly backed by major institutions including the banks. Many factors also provide invoice discounting services.

Leasing companies provide specialist facilities to meet requirements for leasing goods.

Credit insurance companies can guarantee trade bills, and trade debts can be insured with them.

Other short-term facilities are identified under government aid.

Medium-term loans

Medium-term loans are provided mainly by the clearing and other banks. They are widely used, often as part of a package of financial facilities, and range between three and ten years. They are made for a variety of purposes which include buying fixed assets, working capital requirements, financing acquisitions, financing new ventures, and refinancing existing debts. The medium-term loan has become popular primarily because it is not repayable on demand, like an overdraft, but is repayable by a number of instalments over the agreed period of the loan. The pattern of repayment can be tailored to fit the earning capacity of the asset being acquired, or to match the estimated overall cash flow of the business. Repayments may begin immediately, after a short period, after a long period (a 'balloon' loan), or they may be deferred until the end of the loan (a 'bullet' loan). The conditions of the loan are agreed at the outset, and it is not subject to any change of credit policy by the authorities.

The advantages of a term loan to your business are:

- It enables you to get finance on a contractual basis as to both term and amount.
- It enables you to plan future cash flow with greater confidence.
- It insulates against possible government borrowing restrictions which the lender might be forced to impose.
- It provides a straightforward means of reducing borrowings.

134

- It helps to ensure that a proportion of the cash flow is deployed towards the purchase and renewal of assets.

Security for a medium-term loan is normally provided by first legal mortgages over freehold or long leasehold property, since the value of the security is expected to be maintained throughout the period of the transaction.

When a medium-term loan is granted, all terms and conditions are set out in a facility letter establishing the conditions both for the bank and borrower. A term loan attracts a higher rate of interest than that charged for overdrafts, and the rule of thumb often used is to add a quarter of 1 per cent per annum over the rate applied to an overdraft. Banks usually charge an initial fee when a medium-term loan facility is accepted. In addition, a further fee on the undrawn balance may be set if you delay taking up the loan for a period of more than, say, three months. You can repay the loan early but a small penalty may be charged. Alternatively, a bank is entitled to demand repayment of a medium-term loan should you default in the repayment of principal or payment of interest, or if there is a breach of any of the conditions set out in the facility letter or in the form of charge.

Where to get medium-term finance

The main banks are the major providers of medium-term loans. Generally, their loans are provided in amounts of over £5000 for periods of up to ten years. The principal banks also provide other specialist forms of medium-term finance, including instalment credit and leasing, through subsidiary or associated companies.

Merchant banks such as the accepting houses can supply or arrange most forms of medium-term finance for companies, though perhaps rarely providing finance for more than five years out of their own funds. In the main, they are interested in propositions for amounts of £50,000 and more, although the minimum can depend on the circumstances.

Other British and foreign banks are able to provide facilities in the medium-term range. They vary in the minimum sums in which they prefer to deal. Some provide leasing through subsidiaries.

Finance Houses, many of which are subsidiaries of major institutions including the banks, supply all types of instalment credit and leasing, and sometimes other forms of finance as well.

Leasing companies provide specialist facilities to meet businesses' requirements for leasing goods.

Venture capital and other specialist investment institutions are generally concerned with equity finance, but many also provide term loans and other medium-term finance, especially as part of a package.

Government assistance of various kinds, typically in the form of grants, is available in certain circumstances; and loans may be available for some purposes from several public sector bodies.

Long-term loans

Long-term lending refers to finance made available for periods between ten and twenty years. It can be used to buy fixed assets which have a long life, such as major plant and machinery, and to fund the purchase or construction of buildings. Long-term finance can also be used to provide semi-permanent working capital or to purchase other businesses, but the scope for your business may be limited if property assets are already in use in support of bank loans and overdrafts.

Long-term lending, by its nature, involves higher interest rates and fees, and the basis on which these charges are structured varies from time to time with market conditions. Repayments are made on an annual reducing basis, although in some cases lenders may allow an initial 'rest' period of up to two years until the new project begins to produce profits to match your cash flow pattern, though the interest element has to be covered during the 'rest' period. Each loan is secured by specific charges, mainly over freehold or long leasehold property. In the latter case, the unexpired part of the lease will be crucial, and an expiry date will be required well beyond the time the loan is repaid. Furthermore, as the finance granted may be high in relation to the value of the particular property, the lender may ask for additional security which (in the case of companies) may be a floating charge.

Mortgage loans

These are loans for which specific assets in land and buildings are used as security. They are usually for at least twenty years and exceptionally for as long as thirty-five years. About two-thirds of the lender's independent valuation of the property or land is the maximum usually lent. Insurance companies and pension funds often specialize in these loans, preferring a lower limit of at least £50,000, but loans can sometimes be made for smaller amounts, particularly where the potential borrower is a policy-holder. Even if you are not a policy-holder, it is worth investigating special mortgage schemes undertaken by some of these institutions for smaller companies, which are generally in the £15,000 to £25,000 range and are occasionally for as little as £5000. Mortgage brokers may also be able to negotiate mortgage loans against first-class properties but, in order to obtain a long-term loan, the borrower must be in a position to offer the lenders a reasonable prospect of stable earnings in the future, and the assets charged must be readily saleable should the enterprise fail. It is sometimes possible, on introduction through solicitors concerned with the administration of private estates, to obtain a mortgage from the trust funds of such estates available for investment. Building societies do not provide mortgages for industrial companies. Long-term mortgages entail considerable preliminary costs (for example, surveys, valuations, and accounting and legal assistance in drawing up agreements) which are always paid by the borrower. The average cost for loans of up to £50,000 is about 2 per cent of the loan. As with building societies' mortgages, the borrower usually has to agree to make regular payments made up in part of repayment of principal and in part of interest.

You may be able to raise funds on the security of your property by means of an additional mortgage based on the market value. Second mortgages can be used to raise cash when the property, on which a first mortgage has already been secured, has increased in value. Some financial institutions may consider participating in second mortgage finance.

Sale and leaseback

These operations normally relate to property, but sometimes to large items of capital equipment. You may sell a specific major asset to a buyer (generally an insurance company, a pension fund, or a financial institution) and then lease it back on a rental. The lease will usually run for up to twenty-five years. The buyer will need to be satisfied that the rental can be met throughout the term of the lease, so investigation will include the past performance of your business and its future prospects, as well as an independent valuation of the asset. The costs of this and all the legal and accounting costs will be your responsibility. With sale and leaseback, funds are released for use elsewhere in the business and, in the short term, the assets used by you do not change. However, the leased asset no longer belongs to your business and the lease will one day come to an end. As a result, in the case of property, alternative accommodation may have to be sought. Additionally, you no longer enjoy the probable capital appreciation of the property. Another point to consider is that the property will be leased back with provision for the revision of the rental at intervals of time. In effect, careful assessment of all the calculations involved is a critical factor, often depending on how urgently funds are required and the long-term effect of the sale of assets on the future of your business.

Where to get long-term finance

The main banks can provide loans for up to twenty years, often with individually adapted repayment schemes.

Merchant banks such as accepting houses and other issuing houses – with a few exceptions – can arrange the raising of long-term finance. They are often interested in approaches from small companies as well as in propositions concerning very large sums. Their lower limits for loans vary considerably, and often depend on the circumstances of each case.

Insurance companies There are a number of insurance companies prepared to consider requests for long-term finance, including conventional mortgage loans and sale-and-leaseback arrangements. The amounts concerned can vary between £5000 and £1 million, though both these limits are flexible. Further details can be obtained from the British Insurance Association.

Pension funds Some long-term facilities are available from pension funds. The minimum and maximum amounts will vary with the fund approached, and with the circumstances of each case put to them. Pension funds are interested in assisting small as well as large businesses, and details can be obtained from the National Association of Pension Funds.

For property finance in inner city areas, **Inter City Enterprises PLC** – a company set up by clearing banks, insurance companies, and pension funds – identifies and packages development propositions and passes them on to financial institutions for funding.

Venture capital and other specialist investment institutions are mainly concerned with equity finance, but may also provide term loans, especially as part of a package.

Other British and foreign banks provide long-term loans or can arrange for them to be raised, often in foreign currencies. They vary in the minimum sums in which they prefer to deal.

Government assistance, typically in the form of grants, is available in certain circumstances.

Equity capital

Your first step towards raising new equity capital is likely to be the incorporation of your business under the Companies Acts. The equity is then divided into shares, which can be issued or sold to outsiders. Companies are usually formed with limited liability, which means that the maximum loss that the shareholders can make is the amount each has agreed to subscribe for shares. Most companies are private companies, and as such are not allowed to offer shares or debentures for sale to the public at large through public issues. But their shares may be bought and sold privately, and there is no limit to the number of shareholders.

In incorporating a business under the Companies Acts, expert advice is needed to help ensure observance of the correct legal forms. Legal advice is also needed in drawing up the memorandum and articles of association which define what a company can legally do. If these are drawn too narrowly, they can affect its growth in future.

A company selling records and musical tapes in the south of England suffered a series of setbacks during the 1970s. Some of the shops were sold and they merged with a competitor in order to survive. However, even after re-organization, the company was concerned that its margins were too low to support the massive loan it required – especially as the banks' base rates were particularly high at that time. The bank manager suggested that the most beneficial means of progress would occur by equity investment, and the company was horrified that it would have to give up over 20 per cent of its shares. But after the initial shock, the equity arm of the bank explained how the capital base of the company would be strengthened by injecting funds which the company would not have to repay, and which would assist its growth.

The arrangements went ahead and after three years, when the company had established itself firmly – including advertising regularly on television – and sales had grown substantially, the bank floated it on the unlisted stock market. The shares were marked up at a premium. At that point, the bank sold its equity in the company to retrieve its investment, which proved to be a very profitable move. The other shareholders in the company became wealthy overnight, and the business became known on a national scale. If it had ignored the equity opportunity, and doggedly relied on an overdraft attracting high rates of interest, the business might never have survived into the 1980s.

Venture capital

Venture capital institutions invest in the equity of companies not listed on the Stock Exchange and become partners in your business. They look for three types of companies:

1 New or very young 'start-up' businesses.

2 Well managed businesses with good growth prospects if adequate finance is available – expected to be ready for flotation on the Stock Exchange within five years.

3 'Turn-round' situations, that is ailing or failing businesses which can be regenerated by an injection of new management and finance.

Investments involve the lender in high-risk situations – new companies, new technologies, and firms started by people with limited business experience. The relationship with a venture capital institution would be likely to involve (as a partner):

- Mutual trust, respect and understanding.
- Acceptance that the lender will be looking for very high returns on the investment. An overall rate in excess of 30 per cent a year is often quoted for the expected return on the total funds invested. This sort of expected return is required to compensate the venture capitalist for the money lost if the venture fails.
- The realization that the institution will be looking for a way of selling its investment even before it takes the decision whether or not to invest in your business.

The institution expects to make the greater part of its return on the equity portion of the investment, which may be realized when the shares are sold. The main methods are to:

1 Sell to you – which may be impossible if you have insufficient finance available at the time.

2 Float the company on the Stock Exchange.

3 Sell to trade buyers or other investors.

The last two methods would mean the loss of your independence.

Persuading a venture capital institution to invest in your business requires that you present an outstanding case for support, proving that you have a good track record, with skills and experience in successfully managing similar projects, and indicating that you have an above-average chance of turning your plans into reality. Only 1 or 2 per cent of applications prove successful, mainly because the presentation is not strong enough. Allow a great deal of time for preparation, discussion and negotiation, since it may take several months to negotiate support.

Venture loans are used for the following main purposes:

- Purchase, extension or alteration of business premises for own business use.
- The acquisition by takeover of an existing business.
- The purchase of plant, machinery, equipment and vehicles.
- The fitting out and equipping of professional business premises.

They are available for amounts of between £5000 and £250,000.

Development capital

Development capital relates to investment in the equity, supported by loans, of a company which has a good potential for future profitable growth. The obvious disadvantage is the dilution of equity which may be distasteful to you if you have built up the company yourself, or if it is a family firm.

The advantages of development capital are as follows:

- The company's capital structure is strengthened and its gearing and borrowing potential are considerably improved.
- In return for conceding equity, you will receive capital at a very critical stage in development, along with the continual assessment of financial needs and the possibility of further available funds in the future, if justified.
- Contribution by the investing company of its skills and experience in management, marketing and production fields.
- The company's image is improved to trading associates and outside institutions.
- The advice and guidance which is available on the way to public flotation.
- The investing company takes only a minority stake; you retain control even after going public if the investing company agrees in advance to make the whole of its stake available to the market on flotation.
- The company will not be burdened with loan repayments in respect of the equity finance provided, although dividends may be required after the initial years.
- The calibre of the executive appointed to the company is probably higher than you could otherwise have afforded.

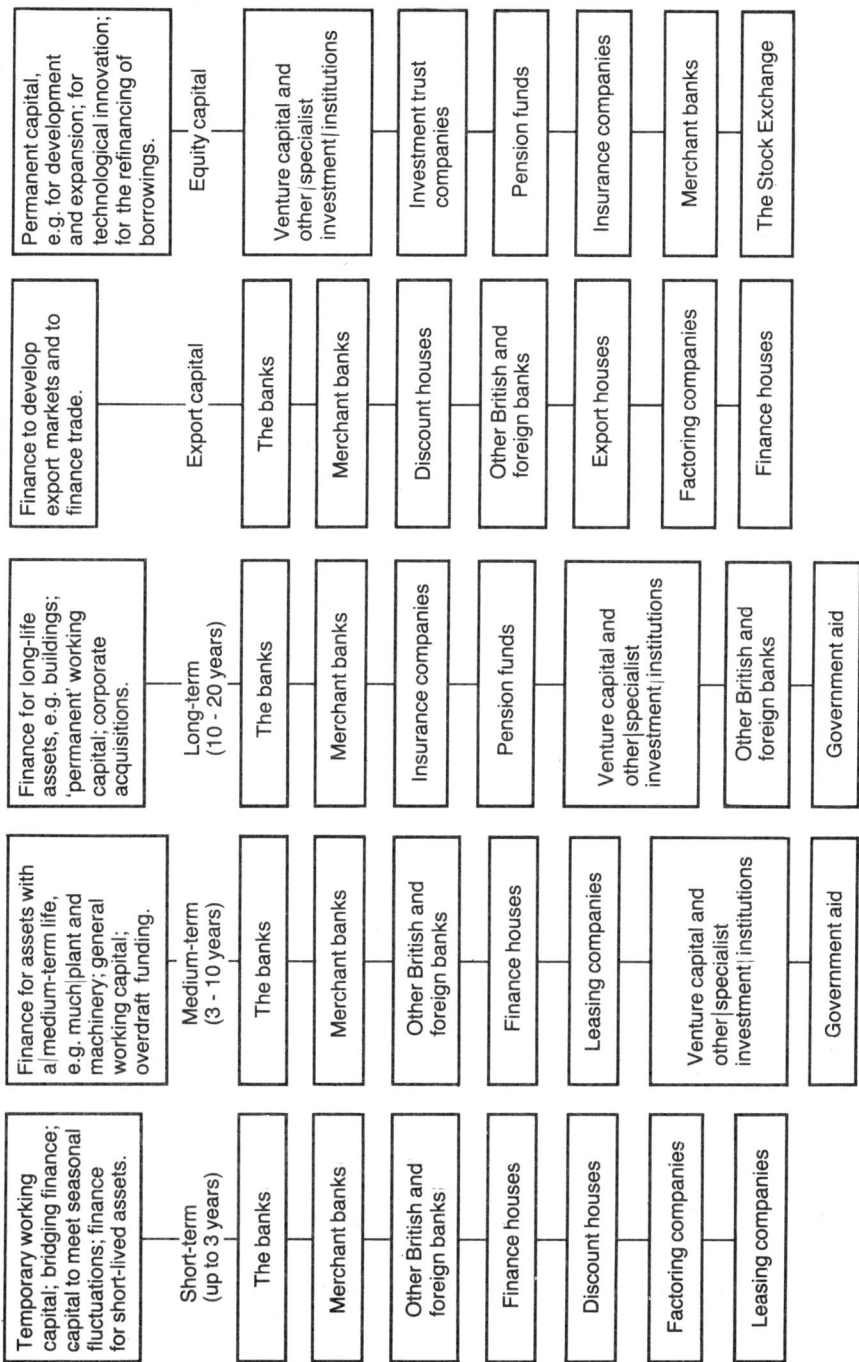

Figure 6 Checklist to sources of finance

Short-term (up to 3 years)	Medium-term (3 - 10 years)	Long-term (10 - 20 years)	Export capital	Equity capital
Temporary working capital; bridging finance; capital to meet seasonal fluctuations; finance for short-lived assets.	Finance for assets with a medium-term life, e.g. much plant and machinery; general working capital; overdraft funding.	Finance for long-life assets, e.g. buildings; 'permanent' working capital; corporate acquisitions.	Finance to develop export markets and to finance trade.	Permanent capital, e.g. for development and expansion; for technological innovation; for the refinancing of borrowings.
The banks	The banks	The banks	The banks	Venture capital and other/specialist investment institutions
Merchant banks	Merchant banks	Merchant banks	Merchant banks	Investment trust companies
Other British and foreign banks	Other British and foreign banks	Insurance companies	Discount houses	Pension funds
Finance houses	Finance houses	Pension funds	Other British and foreign banks	Insurance companies
Discount houses	Leasing companies	Venture capital and other/specialist investment institutions	Export houses	Merchant banks
Factoring companies	Venture capital and other/specialist investment institutions	Other British and foreign banks	Factoring companies	The Stock Exchange
Leasing companies	Government aid	Government aid	Finance houses	

Suitable candidates are private limited companies unable to obtain further finance to expand because of inadequate balance sheet strength and/or lack of security. You should have a first-class management structure, and a sound business plan, as well as above-average growth potential, reflecting particularly the quality of management and its track record, indicating favourable marketing opportunities.

Where to get equity capital

The banks have developed various techniques for providing or securing equity finance for small firms. Most of them have established subsidiaries for this purpose, as mentioned above.

Investment trust companies are often prepared to purchase new shares in industrial and commercial companies. The amount provided depends on the investment trust concerned and the particulars of each case. It may be as low as £25,000 or as high as £750,000. Private as well as public companies can obtain the financial backing of investment trusts.

Pension funds will in some cases consider providing equity finance for smaller companies, and one or two of the nationalized industries' funds have specific schemes for this purpose. The conditions and amounts involved vary with each fund. Details can be obtained from the National Association of Pension Funds.

Insurance companies will sometimes consider applications for equity and development finance from existing and new businesses. Details can be obtained from the British Insurance Association.

Merchant banks have a key role in the equity finance area. They may themselves provide equity or arrange the direct equity finance participation of other financial institutions. Some of these institutions will also support entirely new ventures that have a promising future. They will not only subscribe, or arrange subscription for new shares, but also buy or procure the purchase of shares from existing holders. They play a crucial part in the processes of 'going public' and of subsequently raising additional funds through the Stock Exchange, by advising on the terms and price of public issues, and by arranging their underwriting when necessary.

Other agencies. These will be forwarded by the British Venture Capital Association, Leith House, 47–57 Gresham Street, London EC2V 7EH (Tel. 01 606 8513).

Action Guidelines

1   Assess your financial needs accurately.

_____

_____

_____

_____

2   What kind of borrowing would suit your business?

_____

_____

_____

_____

3   Have another look and check it again!

_____

_____

_____

_____

4   Could bill finance help you?

_____

_____

_____

_____

5   Work out whether you would do better with hire-purchase or leasing than an overdraft or loan.

_____

_____

_____

_____

6   Examine your operations to see whether factoring, invoice discounting or block discounting can help.

_____

_____

_____

7   Could you arrange or re-arrange finance by getting a medium-term
    loan – as well as a small overdraft?

_____

_____

_____

8   Is a long-term loan of use to your business?

_____

_____

_____

9   Can you use a mortgage loan or a sale-and-leaseback arrangement to
    your advantage?

_____

_____

_____

10 Find out the terms of long-term lending from insurance companies.

_____

_____

_____

11 Consider the advantages of venture capital. Assess the future of your
    busines in those terms.

_____

_____

_____

12 Contact all the financial institutions mentioned and then work out the
    type of finance you need and the best terms you can get.

_____

_____

7

How to Get Assistance from the Government, the EEC, and Other Sources

- From whom can you get professional advice for nothing?

- What schemes are available for your business?

- How would you like cheap fixed-rate loans?

- Which locations attract regional development grants?

- Do you know of the schemes that could be of benefit to you?

- Would you like a free factory?

- Where can you get ten-year benefits including exemption from rates?

- Did you know you can get money per capita of staff?

You may have heard about government aid and loans from the EEC. Most business people tend to know so little about them that some marvellous opportunities are missed. Government aid is an Aladdin's Cave with few knowing the word 'Sesame'. There are grants, cheap mortgages, numerous allowances, and a multitude of benefits all waiting for you to apply for them. But first of all you need to have a look at the schemes to find out what is on offer.

Without any doubt you should examine them before you go to a bank for finance. Failure to do so may mean that you can get expensive finance in haste and repent at leisure.

The government is trying hard to encourage small and medium-sized firms to grow and it is offering to help in many ways. It does this mainly through the Department of Trade and Industry and there are very many schemes. It is impossible to outline all of them in detail in one chapter, but the facts set out below give you the most important information which will help you decide whether your business can benefit. Many of the schemes offer grants and free consultancy or advice. Each one has a distinct purpose, and the more you understand the motive behind it the easier access will be. The other point to remember is that most of the assistance offered is available to all small firms, but a number of schemes are limited to certain types or sizes of business or to specific areas of the country.

When you apply for aid, you will need to supply recent accounts, together with a business or project plan, including projected accounts and cash flow forecasts for the next two or three years – or longer if the project is long-term. These should show that the business has good management, adequate manpower, technical skill, and finance to complete the project successfully. The government is likely to want the same amount of information as you will need when making your own decisions on the proposal.

The preparation of a business plan which is then sent to the government will prove to them that the project is fully thought out.

In particular there are a few points to bear in mind:

- The development proposed should not be out of proportion to the size of the firm.
- Product or process proposals should be shown to be technically sound.
- The market for the company's products will have to be identified and well researched.

Many grants and some other forms of government assistance are only available in cases where the aid will make something extra happen which would not occur without it. For example, you may hesitate to make an investment because of certain problems, or perhaps because the economy is weak and markets are slack. The government will help you to finance a project which would otherwise not proceed, or not proceed at so early a date, in order to create jobs in an assisted area of the country, or start up a new enterprise which could not otherwise raise finance, or develop an existing business.

Before becoming involved in the schemes themselves, let us look at some of the advisory services on offer which are absolutely free.

Advisory services

Small Firms Service
This is operated by the Department of Trade and Industry and is designed to improve the availability of information and advice to small firms. Free information is available to you on a wide variety of management questions. It is aimed at existing businesses and at people who wish to start their own business. Counsellors offer sound, practical, impartial and confidential advice on all kinds of business inquiries. In particular, they will help you to draw up a business plan, raise money, choose the right premises, plan your marketing, or reassess production. They can give an impartial opinion or second opinion on your plans if you are concerned and need them to be checked. Three free advisory sessions can be arranged with a counsellor, but after that a nominal fee of £20 is charged for each further session. Apart from the twelve Small Firms Centres, counselling is available at over eighty area counselling offices around the country. All you need to do is dial the operator and ask for Freefone 2444.

Local Enterprise Agencies (LEAs)
These are small local advisory organizations in England, Scotland, Wales and Northern Ireland, usually funded by large companies with local authority support. The range of their services varies but they all aim to provide business advice and counselling for small firms. In addition, some also provide training and managed workshops, or organize business exhibitions and seminars. The

local Small Firms Service will be able to put you in touch with the nearest Local Enterprise Agency.

CoSIRA

The Council for Small Industries in Rural Areas aims to help small firms with technical, management and financial advice and training. CoSIRA can also help you to find premises and raise finance, and can offer technical or management consultancy services. Its head office is at 141 Castle Street, Salisbury (tel. (0722) 336255) but there are local offices in most counties in England. The Small Firms Service will be able to give you the address of the local representative.

Development Agencies

If a business is situated in (or wishes to relocate to) Scotland, Wales or Northern Ireland, there are local agencies which can put you in touch with all the services available and help with finance, training and advice. They are the Scottish Development Agency, the Highlands and Islands Development Board, the Welsh Development Agency, Mid-Wales Development, and, in Northern Ireland, the Local Enterprise Development Unit. (See list of addresses at the end of this book.)

Northern Ireland

Generally, more generous grants are offered in Northern Ireland. You should contact:

- For firms employing over fifty people: Industrial Development Board, IDB House, 64 Chichester Street, Belfast BT1 4JX (tel. (0232) 233233).
- For firms employing less than fifty people: Local Enterprise Development Unit, Lamont House, Purdy's Lane, Newtownbreda, Belfast BT8 4TB (tel. (0232) 691031).

The Department of Economic Development can advise on tourism assistance in Northern Ireland and it also operates a small firms information service. Contact can be made on Freefone 2444 or by telephoning Belfast (0232) 63244.

Technical Enquiry Service

A free advice/consultancy service is offered to small manufacturing businesses which have a technical or production problem. All manufacturers with up to 200 employees are eligible for up to five days of on-the-spot consultancy. Manufacturing includes assembly of a product from purchased components but not repackaging and distribution of a product purchased complete. Contact the Production Engineering Research Association (PERA) on Melton Mowbray (0664) 64133.

Manufacturing Advisory Service

The MAS is designed to provide advice on technical manufacturing problems to 'larger' small firms. It can provide, free of charge, up to fifteen days of consultancy on any subject related to the methods of organization of manufacture. Manufacturing businesses with between sixty and one hundred employees are eligible. Contact the Production Engineering Research Association (PERA) on Melton Mowbray (0664) 64133 and ask for the MAS office. For the North Western Region only, contact Salford University Industrial Centre Limited on (061) 736 8921 and ask for MAS.

Quality Assurance Advisory Service

This is a consultancy offered free of charge to help businesses to obtain quality assurance from a recognized authority. Manufacturing businesses with between sixty and one thousand employees can obtain, free of charge, up to fifteen days of quality assurance consultancy aimed at quality assurance certification by a recognized body. Additionally, up to a further fifteen days are available at half cost. Manufacturing establishments with less than sixty employees can have, free of charge, up to five days of quality assurance consultancy aimed at quality assurance certification by a recognized authority. Contact the Production Engineering Research Association (PERA) on Melton Mowbray (0664) 64133.

Design Advisory Service Funded Consultancy Scheme

This may provide manufacturers with up to fifteen days of free consultancy on all aspects of product design, plus a further fifteen days at half cost. All manufacturers with between sixty and one thousand employees are eligible. Contact the Design Council in London on 01 839 8000 and ask for the Design Advisory Service Funded Consultancy Scheme.

Energy Advisory Services

An energy management programme which will enable firms to reduce their energy costs and lead to increased profits is contained in a series of leaflets entitled 'Profit from Energy Cost Management'. These leaflets, and a range of energy-saving promotional material, posters, stickers and other literature, are available from the Energy Efficient Office (EEO), Room 1312, Thames House South, Millbank, SW1P 4QJ.

Energy Efficiency Survey

Assistance towards the cost of employing an experienced consultant to carry out a survey of energy use may be available under the Energy Efficiency Survey scheme administered by the Energy Efficiency Office. Grants are available for half the cost of the survey up to a maximum of £250 (excluding VAT), and no prior approval is required. Extended Energy Efficiency Survey grants, subject to prior approval from the Department of Energy, are also available for half the cost of the survey up to a maximum of £10,000. Further information and application forms are available from the Energy Efficiency Office, Room 1697 Thames House South, Millbank, SW1P 4QJ (tel. 01 211 3347 or 7074).

Once you have received advice from one of the agencies, you will want to go ahead with your plans. These may concern loans as set out below.

Loans

Loan Guarantee Scheme

No one likes to be turned down when asking for finance, and you may have raised all the finance you can from other sources and still be short of the funds needed to finance your business properly. This scheme is aimed at those propositions where the bank manager believes that the business plan is realistic, but does not feel able to lend, because there is insufficient security or the business has no track record. Another purpose of the scheme is to offer you help without forcing you to mortgage your house or sell other personal assets to raise business finance. A bank is not allowed to take personal security for a government-guaranteed loan, but you will be expected to pledge all the available business assets as security for guaranteed loans. Under this scheme, loans are offered from two to seven years.. Interest rates are set by the lender, with the government also making a charge of 5 per cent for the guarantee. The maximum amount that can be borrowed under the scheme is £75,000. Almost all businesses qualify, as long as a bank manager indicates that he or she would like to make a loan, but could not do so without the benefit of the government guarantee. However, some activities are excluded – agriculture, banking, education, forestry, estate agents, insurance, recreational or cultural services, tied public houses and travel agents.

All you need to do is to complete two simple application forms which the bank will give you, and when completed the bank will pass one to the Department of Trade and Industry who issue the guarantee to the bank. In addition, you are expected to provide the bank with the sort of information required when applying for normal loan finance. This information is not passed to the DTI but is required for the appraisal of the lending proposition carried out by the bank.

Although a borrower under this scheme does not have to offer security, the cost is very high. Rates are set by each lender – competing banks may offer higher or lower rates – and a small business might be charged, say, 3½ per cent over base rate. If base rate is 11½ per cent, the bank will be looking for 15 per cent from you. But you will need to add a further 5 per cent more for the interest required by the government for its guarantee to the bank. So the final rate will be 20 per cent. If you check your margins and calculate your overheads, it is almost certain that you will come to the conclusion that borrowing money at 20 per cent is more than likely to short-circuit your survival. For example, on a loan of £60,000 you would have to pay interest of £12,000 a year. Is it really worth it?

Fixed rate loans from Europe
Although there is often an uncomfortable feeling about borrowing foreign money, the EEC should be considered as a possible cheap and useful source of finance. The European Investment Bank (EIB) and the European Coal and Steel Community (ECSC) can provide medium-term, fixed-rate finance. The loans are for up to

50 per cent of the cost of capital expenditure, with a fixed rate of interest over eight years. The government operates an Exchange Risk Guarantee Scheme to protect you against losses arising from adverse exchange rate movements. This allows the loans to be made in sterling with the government carrying the exchange risk, in return for a small fee based on the outstanding balance of the loan.

EIB loans (including exchange risk cover) are about 2 per cent cheaper than borrowing from UK sources of finance. ECSC loans are available in certain parts of the country on similar terms to EIB lending, but in addition carry a subsidy in the form of an interest rebate of up to 5 per cent for the first five years of the life of the loan. Businesses employing up to 500 people in manufacturing industry or industry-related services throughout the UK are eligible for EIB loans of between £15,000 and £250,000 to finance up to 50 per cent of capital expenditure on a project. Businesses in the service sector, with a wider than local market, will normally be eligible, but local consumer services are excluded. ECSC loans are available to companies employing less than 500 people and creating jobs suitable for ex-coal or ex-steel workers within fifteen miles of a coal or steel closure. Applicants will be expected to satisfy the lender of the commercial viability of their proposal. The procedure for loans of up to £250,000 is relatively simple. For larger projects further information may be needed concerning exchange risk cover. Table 12 sets out organizations operating one or both of these schemes.

Table 12

	EIB	ECSC
DTI Regional Office, Scottish, Welsh & Northern Ireland Offices	Yes	No
Scottish Development Agency	Yes	Yes
Welsh Development Agency	Yes	Yes
Barclays Bank	Yes	Yes
Clydesdale Bank	No	Yes
Co-operative Bank	No	Yes
Industrial & Commercial Finance Corporation (ICFC)	Yes	Yes
Midland Bank	Yes	No
National Westminster Bank	Yes	Yes
Royal Bank of Scotland	No	Yes

Applications for small loans (up to £250,000) can be approved by the EIB within about two weeks of being submitted – sometimes less.

There are other EEC schemes relating to employment and training grants, agricultural guidance and aid, regional grants, finance for energy, and aids for research and development. For free information contact the Department of Industry (tel. (01) 212 0400). (See list of addresses at the end of this book.)

A company in Wiltshire offering an advisory service on energy saving noticed a lucrative gap in the market for a rapid heating element in special areas, such as garages, workshops, hangars, etc. It was decided to manufacture this heating element for sale to the industrial markets, but the project could not proceed without financial assistance. A decision was made to borrow the required funds from the European Investment Bank which offered advantageous rates, and the application was passed to the company's bank manager. Inquiries were made and the company was informed that the loan could not be granted because the location of the factory was not in an Assisted Area. The directors were dissatisfied with the reply and made further inquiries. They discovered that The New Community Instrument or Ortoli facility existed to assist small and medium-sized companies located outside Assisted Areas. They applied for a facility of 50 per cent of the cost of fixed assets, which amounted to £30,000, and obtained a loan for an eight-year term at a fixed rate of interest, which was 11.5 per cent, including the exchange risk cover premium required. In addition, capital repayments were waived for the first two years of the loan. The local bank made all the arrangements with the assistance of its Head Office and within four weeks the project was under way. All funds and repayments were made in sterling, so there were no exchange rate problems for the company.

Grants

There are many grants offered to businesses by the Department of Trade and Industry, some of which may be suitable for your business plans, and could be of great benefit to you.

Support for Innovation (SFI)
This programme intends to improve the technological base of the UK in order to get new or improved products or processes to the market more quickly. The form of support is a grant towards eligible costs. You should approach the Department of Trade and Industry through its Regional Office (or, in Wales, the Welsh Office Industry Department and, in Scotland, the Scottish Office Industry Department) before submitting an application. If the project can be considered, the applicant will be invited to complete an application form and also to supply supplementary information. Although SFI is not designed to provide start-up finance to a new company, newly formed companies are eligible to apply for SFI assistance – this does not apply to sole traders or partnerships.

New technologies
Within the SFI programme special arrangements are announced from time to time to encourage the application of important new technologies. Brief details of the arrangements announced so far are set out below.

Biotechnology To encourage the application of biotechnology in industry, grants are available to help assess opportunities, undertake feasibility studies, or solve particular problems. Businesses in, or closely associated with, the manufacturing sector are eligible. Contact: Department of Trade and Industry, Biotechnology Unit, Laboratory of the Government Chemist, Stamford Street, London SE1 9NQ (tel. 01 928 7900 ext. 601/628).

Computer-Aided Design, Computer-Aided Manufacture (CADCAM) Arrangements are intended to promote the application of computer-aided design and manufacturing techniques in the mechanical and electrical industries. Grants may be available towards the costs of feasibility studies, and the purchase of hardware and software. There are no restrictions on the size or location of eligible companies. Contact: Computer Aided Engineering Data Service, Institution of Electrical Engineers, Savoy Place, London WC2R 0BL (tel. 01 240 8159).

Computer-Aided Design, Manufacture and Test (CADMAT)

To encourage computer-aided design, manufacture and test techniques in the electronics industry, grants are available for research and development of CADMAT tools. Contact: CADMAT Programme Office, Institution of Electrical Engineers, Savoy Place, London WC2R 0BL (tel. 01 240 1871).

Fibre Optics and Opto-electronics Scheme Grants are available for all special plant and equipment necessary for the development and production of new or significantly improved products or processes – in relation to optical fibres, opto-electronics, optical sensors and related instruments. Contact: Department of Trade and Industry, Electronic Applications Division, Room 304, 29 Bressenden Place, London SW1E 5DT (tel. 01 213 5816).

Flexible manufacturing systems Grants may be made available towards the cost of feasibility studies, and towards the development and capital expenditure costs involved in applying flexible manufacturing techniques. There are no restrictions on the size or location of qualifying companies. Contact: Department of Trade and Industry, MEE 1 Branch, Room 530, Ashdown House, 123 Victoria Street, London SW1E 6RB (tel. 01 212 6515).

Industrial robots Grants are made towards development costs up to the point of commercial production. They may also be available towards the costs of feasibility studies and applying robot technology. There are no restrictions on the size or location of qualifying companies. Contact: Department of Trade and Industry, MEE 1 Branch, Room 530, Ashdown House, 123 Victoria Street, London SW1E 6RB (tel. 01 212 0724).

Microelectronics Industry Support Programme Grants and financial support for investment in plant and buildings are available to encourage research and development of new products and processes, and to help with marketing and product launches. There are no restrictions on the size or location of qualifying companies. Contact: Department of Trade and Industry, Electronic Applications Division, Room 306, 29 Bressenden Place, London SW1E 5DT (tel. 01 213 5836).

Software Products Scheme Grants are available towards the cost of developing and marketing innovative computer software products. Proposals may be put forward by a UK-based service company such as a computer software firm, a computer systems firm, a computer bureau or a computer consultancy. Contact: National Computing Centre Ltd, Oxford Road, Manchester M1 7ED (tel. (061) 228 6333).

Clothing, footwear and textiles investment assistance
The government has announced plans to help investment in technologically advanced equipment in the clothing, footwear and textile industries. Grants of up to 20 per cent of the cost of qualifying investment may be available to small firms. Details of the final form of this assistance are available from the Department of Trade and Industry Regional Offices.

Innovation-Linked Investment Scheme Grants are available towards launching new and improved products and processes into production and for conducting market appraisal studies. Applications for production launch assistance are restricted to small and medium-sized firms employing less than 500 people.

Regional Development Grants The purpose of these grants is to encourage manufacturing investment in the Development Areas (DAs) and Special Development Areas (SDAs). The grants are paid in respect of investment in new – not secondhand – physical assets, that is plant, machinery, buildings and works provided for use on qualifying premises in the appropriate areas. Qualifying premises are mainly those involved in manufacturing activities. Once you have qualified, the grant is payable on virtually all assets provided on the premises – excluded are land, residential accommodation and furniture.

Development Areas and Special Development Areas
Those areas which attract this type of grant are as follows:

North West Region: Allerton, Ashton-in-Makerfield, Bedington, Belle Vale, Birkenhead, Bootle, Crosby, Ellesmere Port, Garston, Hindley, Hoylake, Kirkby, Liverpool, Neston, Old Swan, Prescot, Runcorn, St Helens, Skelmersdale, Wallasey, Walton, Widnes and Wigan.

Northern Region: Ashington, Aspatria, Bedlington, Birtley, Blaydon-on-Tyne, Blyth, Chester-le-Street, Cleater Moor, Cockermouth, Consett, Cramlington, Crook, Durham, East Boldon, Eston, Felling, Gateshead, Guisborough, Hartlepool, Houghton-le-Spring, Jarrow and Hebburn, Lanchester, Loftus, Maryport, Middlesborough, Milton, Morpeth, Newburn, Newcastle-upon-Tyne, North Shields, Peterlee, Prudhoe, Redcar, Saltburn, Seaham, Shields Road, South Shields, Southwick, Sperrymoor, Stanley, Stockton and Thornaby, Sunderland, Wallsend, Washington, West Moor, Whitehaven, Whitley Bay, Wingate, Workington, Yarm.

Yorkshire and Humberside Region: Beverley, Bramsholme, Goldthorpe, Grimsby, Hessle, Hull, Mexborough, Rotherham.

South West Region: Bodmin, Bude, Camborne, Camelford, Devonport, Falmouth, Hayle, Helston, Ilfracombe, Launceston, Liskeard, Looe, Newquay, Penzance, Plymouth, Plympton, Redruth, St Austell, St Ives, Saltash, Tavistock, Truro, Wadebridge.

East Midlands Region: Corby.

Scotland: Airdrie, Alexandria, Arbroath, Ayr, Barrhead, Bathgate, Bellshill, Blairgowrie, Blantyre, Bo'ness, Broxburn, Buckie, Cambuslang, Campbeltown, Carluke, Clydebank, Coatbridge, Cowdenbeath, Cumbernauld, Cumnock, Denny, Dingwall, Dumbarton, Dundee, Dunfermline, Dunoon, Easterhouse, East Kilbride, Falkirk, Fort William, Girvan, Glasgow Central, Glenrothes, Govan, Grange-mouth, Greenock, Hamilton, Helensburgh, Hillington, Invergordon, Inverness, Irvine, Johnstone, Kilbirnie, Kilmarnock, Kilsyth, Kilwinning, Kinning Park, Kirkaldy, Kirkintilloch, Lanark, Largs, Larkhill, Lesmahagow, Leven and Methill, Livingston, Lochgilphead, Maryhill, Motherwell, Newton Stewart, Oban, Paisley, Parkhead, Patrick, Port Glasgow, Portree, Renfrew, Rothesay, Rutherglen, Saltcoats, Sangquhor, Shawlands, Shotts, Springburn, Stornoway, Stranraer, Thurso, Troon, Uddingston, Wick, Wishaw.

Wales: Aberdare, Abergavenny, Abertillery, Almwch, Ammanford, Bangor, Bargoed, Barry, Beaumaris, Bethesda, Blackwood, Blaenau Ffestiniog, Cefn Mawr, Cymmer, Ebbw Vale, Ferndale, Fishguard, Flint, Garnant, Haverfordwest, Holyhead, Holywell, Lampeter, Llandyssul, Llangefri, Llantrisant, Llantwit Major, Maesteg, Merthyr Tydfil, Milford Haven, Mold, Neath, Pembroke Dock, Penarth, Penygroes, Pontadawe, Pontlottyn, Pontypool, Pontypridd, Porth

(Tonypandy), Porthmadog, Pwllheli, Resolven, Rhyl, Shotton, Tonyrefail, Tredegar, Treharris, Treorchy, Wrexham, Ystradynlais, Ystrad Mynach.

Regional selective assistance
This assistance takes the form of grants towards the cost of developments or projects (including essential training costs) which will create or preserve jobs in those areas called Assisted Areas. The project or development must be located in the Assisted Areas. Most manufacturing, mining and construction industries are eligible. If a Regional Development Grant is also payable, this will be taken into account when assessing the amount of financial assistance needed for the project to proceed. The majority of the projects assisted are small. Further details and application forms are available from the Department of Trade and Industry or (in Scotland and Wales) from the Scottish and Welsh Offices.

Office and Service Industries Scheme (OSIS)
Special grants are available to service industries based on the number of new jobs a project expects to create over three years in the Assisted Areas. This is available to 'non-manufacturing' activities of all industries (for example, offices, research and development units, training centres) and to service industries covered by the Standard Industrial Classification Orders XXII to XXVI (for example, finance, insurance, etc.), which create jobs in the Assisted Areas. Local consumer-type activities such as retail outlets, high street banking operations, garages, etc., are excluded. Assistance is available to projects of any size.

Tourism assistance
This scheme, designed to encourage the development of tourism, is administered by the English, Scottish and Welsh Tourist Boards. Assistance is usually in the form of a grant towards capital costs, although it may be made in the form of loans or interest relief grants. It is available to all types of tourism projects throughout England, Scotland and Wales, including hotel improvements, leisure amenities, self-catering projects and tourist support facilities. In Scotland and Wales applications should be made to the Scottish or Welsh Tourist Board, and in England to the English Tourist Board. (See list of addresses at the end of this book.)

161

The scheme offers grants for smaller projects with capital costs of between £5000 and £100,000 in eight development categories (holiday centres, tourist information centres, caravan sites, camp sites, farm accommodation, hotels, guest houses and tourist amenities) subject to a maximum grant of 25 per cent. The British Tourist Authority, 64 St James's Street, London SW1A 1NF (tel. 01 629 9191) is able to offer advice on overseas promotions by individual agencies in the UK and to help co-ordinate these where appropriate. It may also offer financial aid towards the cost of such promotions. The Highlands and Islands Development Board (HIDB) can also promote tourism under separate legislation. In Northern Ireland, the Department of Economic Development has overall responsibility for tourism and the Northern Ireland Tourist Board. Several other schemes of government assistance can be of help to the tourism industry: for example, the Urban Development Grant Scheme and the Sports Council and Countryside Commission grants, while local authority tourism projects in the Assisted Areas may apply for European Regional Development Fund grants.

A company in the Midlands involved in leisure activities – pool rooms, squash clubs, and a small health farm – decided to venture into tourism. It identified an area in Wales where it wanted to build a leisure centre and fun park which would be open to the public and attract visitors from the UK and overseas. The directors contacted the Wales Tourist Board with a view to borrowing £120,000 to undertake the project and they were offered the following if the application was successful:

1 Grants and loans up to £200,000 or 49 per cent of the capital expenditure under the Special Tourist Projects Scheme.
2 Loans up to £50,000 or 80 per cent of capital expenditure to develop accommodation, under the Small Establishments Loan Fund, for a term up to twenty years.
3 Interest relief grants based on future cash flow – reducing the cost of borrowing by 3 per cent per annum for up to four years.
4 European Investment Bank loans – up to a maximum of 50 per cent of capital costs.

It was stressed that priority would be given to projects which provided full-time employment opportunities; helped to extend the

162

length of the season; enhanced the range and quality of the facilities and amenities provided; improved social facilities and local infrastructure; and were of good standards of design.

All applications had to be made to the Wales Tourist Board, and the company arranged an advantageous financial package which was far cheaper than any normal form of bank borrowing.

Other assistance

Industrial and commercial premises
The government finances the English Industrial Estates Corporation (trading as English Estates), Kingsway, Team Valley, Gateshead, Tyne & Wear NE11 0NA (tel. (0632) 878941), to provide industrial and commercial premises in the assisted and rural areas of England, and in some other areas where English Estates has been asked to undertake specific initiatives to help stimulate local economic activitiy. This includes office development, derelict land clearance, and the provision of purpose-built units for high technology businesses linked to university facilities, as well as standard factory and warehouse units.

English Estates can offer a full professional design and building service to cater for individual and/or specialist property needs. Land is available to accommodate such development, some of which is located within the Enterprise Zones. Rents for government-financed factories will be determined according to local market conditions, as will the availability of rent-free periods and other rental concessions. Leases can include an option to purchase. Mortgages for the purchase of a factory can be arranged with the main banks at favourable rates, and under guarantee from English Estates, whose offices are located at Gateshead, Consett, Workington, Thornaby, Ripon, Liverpool, Doncaster, Sleadford, Ashbourne, Norwich, Hereford, Bodmin, Exeter, Yeovil and Chatham.

Coal, steel and textile closure areas
Grants of up to 55 per cent of eligible costs over a three-year

163

period are available from what is known as the 'non-quota' section of the European Regional Development Fund (ERDF) to stimulate the provision of services which help new businesses to get started or develop in areas suffering from special industrial restructuring problems. Assistance is limited geographically to:

- Steel closure areas in Strathclyde, Cleveland, Clywd, South and West Glamorgan, and Corby.
- Shipbuilding closure areas in Strathclyde, Tyne and Wear, Cleveland, Merseyside, and Belfast.
- Textile closure areas in Northern Ireland, Tayside, West Yorkshire, Lancashire, and Greater Manchester.

Local authority assistance
Many local authorities are becoming more and more involved in economic development by adopting a wide range of measures designed to encourage industry and employment. Some have premises to offer on industrial estates. Others may provide finance, advice or general information about services in their area. For details, contact the local authority in your area and ask for their industrial or economic development officer. Local authorities in certain inner city areas have been given extra powers under the Urban Programme to help industry and commerce by the provision of loans and grants.

A furniture manufacturer in Kent considered relocation to Merseyside to extend his business, rather than having to buy a new expensive factory. His main problem related to transport costs, as most of his customers were located in the south east of England. He wrote to the Merseyside Development Corporation which offered him the following facilities:

1 A comprehensive range of industrial premises.
2 Rent grants: up to two years' rental grant towards new or existing premises for manufacturing and non-local service industry.
3 Construction grants: up to 50 per cent grant for construction conversion/adaptation of industrial and commercial premises.

4   Interest relief of up to 12 per cent towards the interest on borrowings.
5   Loans: in special cases loans of up to 100 per cent of the capital cost of land acquisition, site clearance, construction of buildings, and the improvement of amenities. Terms are negotiable.
6   Grants of 30 per cent of the average wage of new employees payable for up to twenty-six weeks.
7   Risk capital up to £100,000 from the Merseyside Enterprise Fund.
8   Grants of 22 per cent in respect of plant and machinery.
9   Loans from the European Investment Bank.
10   Aid from the European Regional Development Fund.

He decided to move and bear the transport costs in line with a sound business plan of development. So he took advantage of many of the grants and loans offered, providing work opportunity for seventy employees.

Enterprise Zones
The government has set up a number of Enterprise Zones (EZs) which will last for ten years. The aim is to encourage industrial and commercial businesses to set up in these zones by offering certain tax concessions and by cutting back certain administrative controls. The individual sites vary widely, but all contain land ripe for development. In size they range from about 55 to 450 hectares.

The seventeen Enterprise Zones in England are in:

Corby	Salford/Trafford
Dudley	Scunthorpe
Glanford (Flixborough)	Speke (Liverpool)
Hartlepool	Telford
Isle of Dogs	Tyneside
Middlesbrough	Wakefield
North East Lancashire	Wellingborough
North West Kent	Workington
Rotherham	

There are three zones in Wales – Delyn, Milford Haven Waterway, and Lower Swansea Valley; three in Scotland – Clydebank, Invergordon and Tayside; and two in Northern Ireland – Belfast and Londonderry.

The following benefits are available for a ten-year period from the date on which each zone is designated:

1 Exemption from rates on industrial and commercial property.

2 Exemption from Land Development Tax.

3 100 per cent allowances for corporation and income tax purposes for capital expenditure on industrial and commercial buildings.

4 Employers are exempt from industrial training levies and from the requirement to supply information to Industrial Training Boards.

5 Simplified business planning – developments that conform with the published scheme for each zone will not need planning permission.

6 Controls in force will be administered more speedily.

7 Applications from firms in EZs for certain customs facilities will be processed as a matter of priority, and certain criteria will be relaxed.

8 Government requests for statistical information will be reduced.

Further information on EZs can be obtained from ICD3, Department of the Environment, Room P2/102, 2 Marsham Street, London SW1P 3EB (tel. 01 212 3434).

Freeports
A freeport is an enclosed zone within (or adjacent to) a seaport or airport where goods are treated for customs purposes as being outside the customs territory of the country. In general, customs duties and agricultural levies are due only when goods are consumed within the zone, or when they cross the perimeter of the freeport area heading for markets in the UK, or in other member states of the European Community. Traders registered for VAT purposes may import goods into a freeport without accounting for tax on them. VAT will become chargeable if goods are removed from the zone for use in the UK. The normal VAT rules will apply to

goods and services supplied to or within the zone. Relief from excise duty will be limited to the bonded warehousing facilities available under existing legislation. The government has designated, on an experimental basis, freeports at the following places:

Belfast Airport	Liverpool
Birmingham Airport	Prestwick Airport
Cardiff	Southampton

Potential users of freeports should contact the appropriate freeport operators.

Employment opportunity schemes

Enterprise Allowance Scheme
This scheme is designed to help unemployed people create their own jobs by setting up in business. It helps by paying an Enterprise Allowance of £40 a week for a year, which compensates them for the loss of unemployment or supplementary benefit that would otherwise occur when starting a business. Expert business advice is also provided by the Small Firms Service of the Department of Trade and Industry. Applicants must be over the age of 18 and under retirement age and have been unemployed or under formal notice of redundancy for at least thirteen weeks. They should be receiving unemployment or supplementary benefit at the time of application, and be able to show that they have access to £1000 to invest in the new business. The allowance is not available to people already operating a business.

Young Workers Scheme
This scheme is designed to encourage employers to recruit more young people under the age of 18 and in their first year of employment into permanent full-time jobs at realistic wage rates. Employers able to fulfil the scheme's conditions and whose gross average weekly wage for such young people is £50 or less may claim a flat-rate reimbursement of £15 a week for each qualifying employee. Young people must be at least 16 years old and have been out of full-time education for at least one year or have left full-time education on or after their 17th birthday.

Job Splitting Scheme

This is designed to encourage employers to split existing full-time jobs into two part-time jobs and so provide more opportunities for unemployed people. A grant of £750 will be paid for each existing full-time job which is split, with an instalment of £300 being paid immediately an application is approved. The remainder is paid in three equal amounts after six months, nine months and twelve months. The scheme is open to all employers. Application and claim forms are available from regional offices of the Department of Employment which can provide full details.

Job Release Schemes

These are special employment measures to create additional jobs for unemployed people. By providing a weekly allowance, the full-time scheme makes it easier for employees nearing state pension age to give up work completely – earlier than they would normally retire. The part-time scheme gives employees near state pension age the opportunity to approach retirement gradually by giving up half their jobs in return for approximately half the allowance paid under the full-time scheme. With both schemes the resulting vacancy must be filled by an unemployed person and the allowance is payable until state pension age is reached. Application forms are available from Department of Employment offices, together with full details of the schemes, including the arrangements for processing applications.

Information on these schemes may be obtained from Department of Employment offices.

Alternative methods of raising finance

Business Expansion Scheme (BES)

Businessmen will usually invest as much as possible of their own capital in their business. Recent changes in income tax and in capital taxes have encouraged potential entrepreneurs to make this sort of investment.

The Business Expansion Scheme was introduced to encourage individual outside investors to provide additional full-risk equity for unquoted trading companies. It is intended to help in meeting the particular needs of new and expanding companies for additional equity where companies do not have ready access to other sources of outside capital. The Business Expansion Scheme offers individual investors income tax relief at their highest rates of income tax for qualifying investment of up to £40,000 a year. Companies are eligible if they are:

* Unquoted.
* Carrying on a qualifying business wholly or mainly in the UK.
* Not controlled by another company, and not controlling other companies except 100 per cent subsidiaries which themselves would qualify.

The main exclusions are activities like leasing and hiring, dealing in shares and land, provision of legal and accounting services, farming and financial investment (for example, in commodities). These apart, the scheme covers a wide range of ordinary manufacturing and service companies. Companies are not excluded if they export some or even all of their output, provided the bulk of their activities is in the UK.

Investment funds can also come within the scheme. Fund managers act as nominees for investors, putting their money into one or more companies chosen by them at the time. But the investor is the beneficial owner of the shares and the conditions are otherwise the same. Further information about the Business Expansion Scheme is available from Tax Districts, PAYE Enquiry Offices and Small Firms Service – ask for leaflet IR51. Companies wishing to seek investments under the Business Expansion Scheme are advised to approach their Inspector of Taxes to check that they meet the qualifying conditions and that the shares will be qualifying shares.

BES investments, however, may create some serious constraints. For example, if a company wishes to remain a 'qualifying' company within the meaning of the legislation, it cannot have overseas subsidiaries. It is not allowed to control another company, other than a qualifying subsidiary which must be wholly-owned. Further, it cannot seek a public stock market quotation for three years

169

following the issue of shares to BES investors. There may be other problems if income is derived from royalties or licence fees which are not considered sufficient to allow the company to qualify for this scheme. These constraints may put a significant brake on the growth of a business, especially if it operates in a technology-related area, and the penalty of circumventing the rules is that the investors stand to lose their tax relief. A further shortcoming of the scheme is that it is highly seasonal. The mechanism and timing of tax relief for investors means that at certain times of the year it may be difficult to obtain funds. Perhaps of widest importance is the emphasis some fund managers may place on the degree of risk they are prepared to take in any one company or, if they are overexposed, in particular industries.

Purchase of own shares – selling an equity stake which is bought back later

Companies may buy back their own shares, which is useful in a scheme where, say, a family business needs equity from outside investors but the owners are keen not to lose control of the business permanently. Companies and shareholders may contract in advance that the shareholders will be bought out in, say, five or seven years' time. Hence, full control of the company is retained and the minority investor has the assurance that his money will not be 'locked in' indefinitely. Any gain made by the shareholder is taxed as a capital gain rather than as a distribution by the company to the shareholder, so long as certain conditions are met. As such, the transaction is not subject to advance corporation tax in the hands of the company or income tax in the hands of the shareholder.

The main points to watch are that the company must have the power to buy its shares in its articles, and that the purchase of the shares must be approved by a special resolution on which the shareholder to be bought out may not vote. In the case of a private company, the funds needed to buy the shares need not come out of retained profits but could, for instance, come from its capital or be borrowed, as long as the company is solvent after the transaction. The legislation is, therefore, very flexible, while safeguarding the interests of creditors. It can be particularly useful in providing an investor under the Business Expansion Scheme with a way out after the five-year qualifying period. But the following conditions must be fulfilled:

- The shareholder must be a resident of the UK.
- The shareholder must have held the shares for at least five years.
- Immediately after the purchase, the shareholder must not hold more than a 30 per cent interest in the business.

Professional advice will be necessary to make sure that the option to buy back the shares meets the conditions set out in the Companies Acts, and you should discuss the matter with your local tax office in advance to obtain the ncessary approval.

Schemes and services available to different types of small business

Manufacturing businesses
New businesses: Loan Guarantee Scheme; Business Expansion Scheme; Employment schemes; Support for Innovation; Regional Development Grants; Regional Selective Assistance/Office and Service Industries Scheme; Small Firms Service; Technical Enquiry Service; Quality Assurance Advisory Service; English Estates premises.

Firms employing less than sixty people: Loan Guarantee Scheme; Business Expansion Scheme; Support for Innovation; Regional Development Grants; Regional Selective Assistance/ Office and Services Industries Scheme; European Community Loan; Small Firms Service; Technical Enquiry Service; Quality Assurance Advisory Service; English Estates premises; Assistance with exports.

Firms employing over sixty people: Loan Guarantee Scheme; Business Expansion Scheme; Support for Innovation; Regional Development Grants; Regional Selective Assistance/Office and Services Industries Scheme; European Community Loan; Manufacturing Advisory Service; Quality Assurance Advisory

171

Service; Design Advisory Service; English Estates premises; Assistance with exports.

Retail service businesses (shops, public houses, etc.)
New businesses: Loan Guarantee Scheme; Business Expansion Scheme; Employment schemes; Small Firms Service.

Firms employing less than sixty people: Loan Guarantee Scheme; Business Expansion Scheme; Small Firms Service.

Firms employing over sixty people: Loan Guarantee Scheme; Business Expansion Scheme.

Other service businesses (including construction)
New businesses: Loan Guarantee Scheme; Business Expansion Scheme; Employment schemes; Regional Selective Assistance/ Office and Service Industries Scheme; Small Firms Service.

Firms employing less than sixty people: Loan Guarantee Scheme; Business Expansion Scheme; Support for Innovation; Regional Selective Assistance/Office and Service Industries Scheme; European Community Loan; Small Firms Service; Assistance with exports.

Firms employing over sixty people: Loan Guarantee Scheme; Business Expansion Scheme; Support for Innovation; Selective Financial Assistance/Offices and Services Industries Scheme; European Community Loan; Assistance with exports.

Action Guidelines

1   List the advisory services available to you and their telephone
    numbers for easy reference.

_____

_____

_____

_____

2   Consider the Loan Guarantee Scheme if you are starting up and
    cannot get finance. Work out how much it will cost you and whether
    you can afford to borrow at that rate.

_____

_____

_____

_____

3   Refer back to the loans offered by EIB and ECSC. How well do they
    fit into your borrowing plans?

_____

_____

_____

_____

4   Review the grants available to your business and get more
    literature from the Department of Trade and Industry.

_____

_____

_____

_____

5   List the Development and Special Development Areas that seem
    attractive to you.

_____

_____

_____

_____

_____

6   Check with the Department of Trade and Industry the benefits of
    Regional Selective Assistance.

_____

_____

_____

_____

7   Consider factory purchase through English Estates.

_____

_____

_____

_____

8   Re-examine the coal, steel and textile closure areas for
    your business.

_____

_____

_____

9   Contact local authorities regarding assistance.

_____

_____

_____

10 Consider the Enterprise Zones and the amenities offered there.

_____

_____

_____

11 Which Employment Opportunity Schemes would be useful for
    your business?

_____

_____

_____

12 Think about the Business Expansion Scheme and look at the details
    again. Note how you can buy back your own shares.

_____

_____

_____

8

How to Obtain Export Finance

- How can you increase your profits by exporting?
- Where can you get information?
- Which markets do you want to expand in?
- Who is giving so much help for free?
- Who will handle your business abroad?
- How will you get payment?
- What guarantees do you have on the safety of your goods abroad?

Selling Overseas

You are probably aware that selling goods abroad is often far more complex than selling to the home market. Yet if you wish to find new markets and increase profits you may have to find outlets abroad if it widens your trading range and offers potential. Exporting is not as difficult as you may think, and much of the mystique will disappear as we go step-by-step through the procedures. Furthermore, a great deal of help will be offered to you by many organizations – and much of it will be free!

It is no secret that in exporting there are problems regarding the language, the legal system and trade customs which are all different, and there may be a greater risk of non-payment than when trading in the UK. In addition, the time taken for goods to pass from the seller to the buyer is generally longer with exports

175

than for goods sold at home. This poses a problem because buyers prefer not to pay until they have examined the goods, while suppliers prefer payment on or before shipment. Exporting also involves payment in a currency foreign either to the buyer or to the seller, or to both; and there are exchange rate risks. Any movements in the values of currencies which take place between the date a contract is signed and the final payment will mean that the seller obtains less (or more) in terms of his own currency than expected; or that the buyer has to pay more (or less) than planned; while exchange control regulations may exist in both the seller's and the buyer's country. However, you may find that these problems are more formidable in print than in practice because there are arrangements and safeguards to protect you from loss.

But before you aim for foreign markets there are a number of factors to assess, and you can obtain advice on how to set about doing so. The things you need to know are:

1   What is the demand (or potential demand) for your products, bearing in mind local tastes, local traditions and even climatic conditions?

2   Who are the competitors – especially those selling under well-established brand names?

3   What will be the most effective – or even acceptable – method of presentation, that is, design and packaging? In some countries this demands a knowledge of local, political, national or religious attitudes.

4   What language is to be used in brochures, packaging, sales and service literature, and in correspondence with potential buyers?

5   Should you advertise and, if so, what media should be used and what will be the cost?

6   What are the means and costs of distribution?

7   Are the products priced competitively in relation to similar goods and to local market conditions?

8   What rating is given to the reputation and soundness of overseas buyers and/or agents?

9   What is the degree of local political stability and commercial efficiency, or the state of the national economy?

10 What is the extent of import restrictions, tariffs and exchange controls?

Markets and information

Finding a market for your product can entail a considerable amount of work and research. Obviously you will want to carry out some basic market research of your own, and you can do so from easily accessible sources. These may be as follows:

Published sources

National newspapers and periodicals contain much up-to-date information, especially in their business supplements, and there is no shortage of reference books from trade organizations. Directories and catalogues contain a wealth of information about markets, competitors and customers: many are available in public libraries. One of the most useful public sources of general information for market research is the Statistics and Market Intelligence Library, housed at the Department of Trade in London. Statistics are an excellent guide to market prospects and can offer you an easy reference to principal overseas markets. The Overseas Trade Statistics of the UK, published by Her Majesty's Stationery Office each month, gives a breakdown of UK imports and exports by product, and their principal countries of origin and destination. The Statistics of Foreign Trade, published by the Organization for Economic Co-operation and Development, gives details of trade between the OECD countries. Listed by product and trading partners, they give an excellent picture of a variety of markets.

Information from your bank

Whether you are new to trading abroad or a well-established international business, you need to be kept informed. Your bank's international teams travel widely and regularly and, in conjunction with representatives resident in key centres of the world, they provide up-to-date news and background information about trading conditions and regulations in all countries. Your bank probably produces regular bulletins which give details of most of the UK's major export markets. Each country is examined in terms of economic and social structure and situation, market opportunities and import requirements; and advice on market entry and setting up in the foreign country is also included. The bulletins are usually offered free of charge.

Your bank will also answer questions about import and export procedures, licensing, tariffs, customs, foreign exchange, methods of payment, documentation, taxation, and finance, and also supply status reports on the commercial standing of companies abroad, so that you can obtain the information you need.

The banks operate Overseas Trade Promotion Departments which try to match agents and companies with businesses in Britain. It is possible to obtain details from them of opportunities in other countries segregated into their separate industry segments. As a result, a potential exporter involved in, say, engineering might forge links with companies in Italy, Spain, Brazil or Indonesia. The service offered by the banks for such matching is usually free – they expect to obtain their reward from the business that follows.

Other sources
The UK is particularly well endowed with organizations which are capable and anxious to give advice and practical help on numerous aspects of importing, exporting and other international business ventures for both existing and potential exporters. The British Overseas Trade Board (BOTB) has various schemes especially designed to help you. The BOTB is responsible for co-ordinating and directing the UK's export promotion services, and its members are businesspeople drawn from public and private sectors of industry, commerce and finance. It is financed by government funds and many of its services are free or subsidized.

If you become involved in international trade you may feel the need for further practical help, and the International Chamber of Commerce produces publications that can be of real service. Its booklet, ICC Publications, lists many of these. Many of the chambers of commerce, trade associations and export houses have international connections and are able to provide an extensive range of services, promotional opportunities and information about prospects in markets abroad. For information about UK chambers of commerce contact the Association of British Chambers of Commerce. If your business is concerned with European countries, then one of the many chambers of commerce based in Europe will be able to assist you. For an address list contact the Council of British Chambers of Commerce in Continental Europe. The British Export Houses Association will be able to put you in touch with export houses in the UK. There are also many export clubs throughout Britain whose members are businesspeople with a wealth of exporting experience. The CBI Central London Export Club will be able to advise you about them. In your search for export contacts, *The Directory of Export Buyers in the UK*, published by Trade Research Publications, will help you. It lists products, export firms based in the UK, and a country-by-country breakdown of the firms dealing with each foreign country. There is also a wide variety of trade organizations, so, whatever business you are in, there is one which can help you. The Confederation of British Industry will be able to suggest the organization best suited to your needs.

It must be pointed out that, although substantial help will be offered to your business by organizations and agencies, at the end of the day you will have to co-ordinate everything if you intend to be successful. Another point is to recognize the importance of management control in exporting as well as in trading at home.

Methods of selling

You are most likely concerned about the methods by which you can sell abroad for your particular business. These may be listed under two headings, selling direct, and selling indirect; the second category is extensive.

Selling direct
This may be carried out if you are in one of the specialist fields of engineering, equipment and instrumentation manufacture, etc., in which your know-how and expertise are required in the sales negotiations; or if you are in the consumer goods field dealing with buying agencies acting on behalf of chains of supermarkets and hypermarkets. Otherwise direct selling is hard work, and can create many problems.

Selling indirect

Agents An agent administers the sales in overseas countries. It may be a firm which can organize every aspect of distribution over a defined area, or an individual seeking buyers for the company. Great care is needed in appointing agents as they will probably be entirely responsible for the success of a business in their territories. The banks, the British Overseas Trade Board (BOTB) and chambers of commerce will help you to appoint an agent. The candidate may be an import commission agent, a stocklist–wholesaler (who is perhaps also the manufacturer of a complementary product line), an import merchant, or a large retailer. Whatever the type of concern – and there are other possibilities – the same points must be considered most carefully. The prospective agent should:

- Preferably be already trading in the same field of business or in a related one.
- Not represent a competitor, or a near or potential competitor.
- Not already have more agencies than can be properly handled.
- Have the financial, staff and other resources to take on the new business in addition to existing commitments.
- Have a good knowledge of local market conditions, especially of fiscal and import licence policies currently in operation.
- Have acceptable banker's and trade references.
- Enjoy a good reputation in the trade and generally in the business community.
- Be a registered agent/distributor where local government legislation makes this a necessary prerequisite to negotiating on behalf of an overseas firm.
- Share an enthusiasm for the business proposed.

You should ensure that a good business relationship can be established with the agent, with a clear understanding on trading practice and procedure, including terms of business, selling and promotion methods, after-sales service, the handling of documents, the payment of commissions, the frequency of visits – in both directions – and periodic reports. Good two-day communication is at the very heart of first-class principal/agent relationships. Once appointed, an agent is protected by law and cannot easily be dismissed. It is essential to find out in detail precisely how an agent's rights are protected and the terms of the agreement.

It should cover, at least, the period of the agreement, provision for ending it, which country's laws will govern it, the extent of the territory, the range of products and services, arrangements for paying commission on sales, and the rate applicable. The relationship should be mutually on trial for some months at least, and it may, in some cases, be prudent to provide for this in a probation clause in the agency agreement. If a trial arrangement as such is intended by both parties, then the tentative character of the arrangement and an agreed period of notice of termination should be clearly stated. It is sometimes difficult, especially in certain countries, for a selling principal to part with an agent, except at considerable expense and even at risk of alienating the local government and business community.

Foreign buying houses in the UK Certain large American and Canadian retail stores have buying agencies in the UK through which they buy the bulk of their British goods. These houses deal with all the formalities and documentation, provide after-sales service and carry the credit risks on foreign buyers. They become virtually another UK customer and the supplier is relieved of all the routine work. Accounts are settled direct in the UK, so your financial risks are minimized and your cash flow protected.

Confirming houses These act as buying agents for an importer to find suppliers of those goods the importer wishes to buy. A manufacturer will deal direct with the confirming house which will usually pay for the goods and often attend to the necessary documentation and shipment.

Export merchants in the UK These buy goods direct from manufacturers. The transaction is almost the same as selling in the home market. Therefore, a company need not carry out market research or find buyers. However, a manufacturer will have no control over the marketing, or the subsequent success or otherwise of the product.

Import houses overseas These import goods to their own country and sell them there. A manufacturer selling goods to an import house will normally have to undertake the shipment and documentation. The marketing is controlled by the import house.

Profitable trade overseas depends very much on selecting the best markets to enter through the right agency. But there is often a temptation to try and sell in as many overseas markets as possible – it is one that should be resisted strongly. By concentrating marketing resources in a few carefully selected areas, you can maximize total profit on sales rather than spreading your investment over a wider area too thinly. One of the best ways to make sure that your sales effort is targeted at the most profitable areas is to carry out a full study of the most likely market for your products. This should be done before you attempt any sales drive into new markets abroad.

After you have found your market, the next stages are documentation, methods of payment, ECGD insurance and freight forwarding.

Documentation

Documentation is a very complicated matter and you should consult with your bank or financial institution at a very early stage to make sure you get everything right from the start. Otherwise, serious problems occur which could affect your business progress as set out in your plan.

With each consignment you will need a bill of lading, which is a receipt for goods upon shipment, a contract and a document of title. It will be signed by an authorized person on behalf of the ship owner, who undertakes to deliver the goods at their destination. Bills of lading include a brief description of the goods, a statement of the terms on which they are to be carried, the name of the carrying vessel, and the name of the port of discharge. They are issued and signed, usually in sets of three, and are important documents because they prove ownership. The overseas buyer needs the bills of lading to clear the goods at his end, and you must make sure that they are available before the goods arrive at the foreign port. You should make out the bills of lading 'to order', as the shipper, and endorse them in blank to complete their transferability. Unlike bills of lading, air consignment notes, parcel post receipts, forwarding agent's receipts, and railway consignment notes are not documents of title.

Commercial invoices are needed by the overseas buyer and must contain the correct information. Generally, this includes a statement of the nature of the contract, a description of the goods, and their price. Most countries specify the information they want to be shown on invoices, such as details of import licences and exchange permits. Invoices are normally addressed to the overseas buyer and should include the shipping marks which appear on the packages and on the bills of lading. Often specifications, which are detailed schedules of the merchandise, and weight lists must accompany the invoices.

Customs invoices in the form required by the authorities of the importing country are usually needed, and sufficient copies should be provided for the use of the customs authorities abroad. A certificate of origin is a declaration stating the country of origin of the goods shipped. In some cases the declaration has to be authenticated by a chamber of commerce. This declaration of origin is often incorporated into the customs invoice.

Consular invoices are mandatory when shipping to certain parts of the world, for example South America. They are specially printed documents which must be completed, together with a visa, by the consulate of the importing country. The forms are available from consuls, chambers of commerce, and shipping or forwarding agents. A Certificate of Inspection may be needed for the shipment of non-perishable goods, and a certificate of health is normally required when livestock or animal products are shipped. A blacklist certificate may also be needed to prove that the goods did not originate in, or were not transported through, blacklisted countries.

The importance of making sure that the documents for transport are complete, accurate and properly and promptly processed cannot be overemphasized. Failure to do so can be very costly. Efforts have been made to standardize and simplify export documentation and procedures, particularly by the Simplification of International Trade Procedures Board (SITPRO). Several thousand exporters use the documentation system introduced by SITPRO which makes possible the production of almost all the export documents from a single master document, thus cutting costs, eliminating repetitive typing and checking, and bringing all the advantages of standardization. Details of this system and other services can be obtained from SITPRO, Almack House, 26–28 King Street, London SW1Y 6QW (tel. 01 214 3399).

It is important that you have complete insurance cover against loss or damage which may occur during shipment. The contract must clearly state who is responsible for arranging the insurance at all stages from the time when the goods leave the exporter's hands until the buyer takes possession. The stages to be covered include:

- Transportation of the goods to the docks or the airport.
- Time during which they are stored awaiting shipment or loading.
- Periods while on board the ship or aircraft.
- Off-loading and storage on arrival.
- Transportation to the buyer.

You should bear in mind the need for an extension to the policy in case of delay at any stage.

Methods of payment

There are many means by which payment can be made which are rather different from normal UK trading operations, and you should note them carefully.

Advance payment

The greatest security which you can get is advance payment of the full contract value – also known as cash with order. It requires the buyer to extend credit to you – a practice usually unattractive to the buyer who has no guarantee that the goods will arrive or, if they do, that they will be in a satisfactory condition. For this and

184

other reasons, advance payments are rarely used.

Open account
This method offers least security to you. The documents of title are sent direct to the buyer who agrees to pay at a certain time – generally according to the terms of payment as laid down in the conditions of sale. Under the arrangement, you lose control both of the goods being exported and of title to them. A high degree of trust in the importer is needed, and this occurs where a good relationship has been established over several years. Settlement can be arranged as follows:

- **Cheque** The buyer could draw a cheque payable at his own bank and send it to the exporter. It may take some weeks to clear through the banking system, although it is sometimes possible to obtain funds against the cheque by having it negotiated at a bank.

- **Banker's draft** This is a cheque drawn by the buyer's bank. Normally, the buyer will send the draft to you, and you can obtain payment through your own bank.

- **Mail transfer (MT)** In this case, the buyer's bank sends instructions by airmail to a bank asking it to credit you or your bank with sterling or foreign currency.

- **Telegraphic transfer (TT)** This is identical to mail transfer except that the instructions are sent by telex, cable or the SWIFT (Society for Worldwide Interbank Financial Telecommunications) network.

Bills of exchange
These provide a very flexible method of settling international trade transactions. They may be 'at sight', where the buyer has to pay cash on presentation of the bill, or 'term/usuance' bills, which offer a credit period to the buyer who signifies agreement to pay on the due date by writing his acceptance across it. Figure 7 shows a specimen bill of exchange.

In the simplest case, you hand a bill of exchange to your bank, which in turn sends it to a bank in the buyer's country where payment is obtained. Documents may be released against

Figure 7 *A specimen bill of exchange*

No.	6/1	1 October	1985 For	£1,960.76

At _____ SIGHT _____ Pay this FIRST of Exchange

_____ to the Order

of _____ OURSELVES, THE SUM OF _____

ONE THOUSAND NINE HUNDRED AND SIXTY POUNDS AND 76 PENCE ONLY

value __ in merchandise shipped to _____ which place to Account

Brazil Invoice No. 18862

To __ Credit Lyonnais,

84-94, Queen Victoria Street,

London EC4P 4LX

For and on behalf of
Jacksonite Twiddle & Co. Ltd.

Authorised Signatory

acceptance or payment according to your instructions. The foreign
bank usually retains the bill of exchange once it has been
accepted and presents it for payment on the due date. Proceeds
are then sent to you in accordance with the instructions of
the buyer's branch. Your bank will help you with this means
of payment.

Promissory notes
A promissory note is simply a promise to pay. It is written by the
buyer promising to pay you an amount of money at a specified
time.

Documentary letter of credit
This is issued by the buyer's bank in accordance with the payment
terms of your contract; it is a guarantee of payment by that bank.
However, you would be well advised to seek advice on the value
of the foreign bank's guarantee, as there may be exchange control
problems, political risks, or even concern regarding the credit
standing of the foreign bank.

If the credit is made irrevocable, the foreign bank is unable to amend
or cancel its terms without the consent of all parties. Further security
can be obtained by you if the bank through which the letter of

credit is transmitted confirms this fact, making it a confirmed irrevocable letter of credit. As payment is then guaranteed by two banks it is the safest method of payment. Subsequently, you are responsible for presenting the appropriate documents to the advising bank. Documentary credits may call for bills of exchange to be either 'at sight' or 'at term'. If it is 'at sight' and is drawn on the advising bank, you will receive payment in cash from that bank on production of the relevant documents. If the bill is 'at term', and an acceptance credit facility has been arranged under an irrevocable letter of credit, the advising bank accepts it, enabling you to sell it for cash at a discount. When the bill matures (usually within 180 days), the holder obtains payment from the advising bank which is then reimbursed through the foreign bank by the overseas buyer. It is essential that the documents relating to a documentary letter of credit conform in all details to the requirements therein, as discrepancies in the documents may result in non-payment. See Figure 8 for an illustration of how documentary credits work.

Goods on consignment
You can ship goods on a consignment basis. In this case there is no specific sales contract, and payment is made by the agent only when the goods have been sold. A bank can arrange for the goods to be stored and insured, either in its own name or in the name of a foreign bank. The goods are then released to the agent only on an undertaking to pay for them from the proceeds of the sale. This system ties up working capital in stocks held abroad, involves insurance and storage expenses, and can carry the risk of confiscation.

Factoring
Factoring is a service being used more and more by exporters who, through the growing level of competition in overseas trade, need to extend open credit terms to foreign customers. A factor buys trade debts and takes over these problems for you for a specific charge.

Acceptances
Acceptance credits are widely used as a means of financing the production and sale of goods for export. They are usually for a

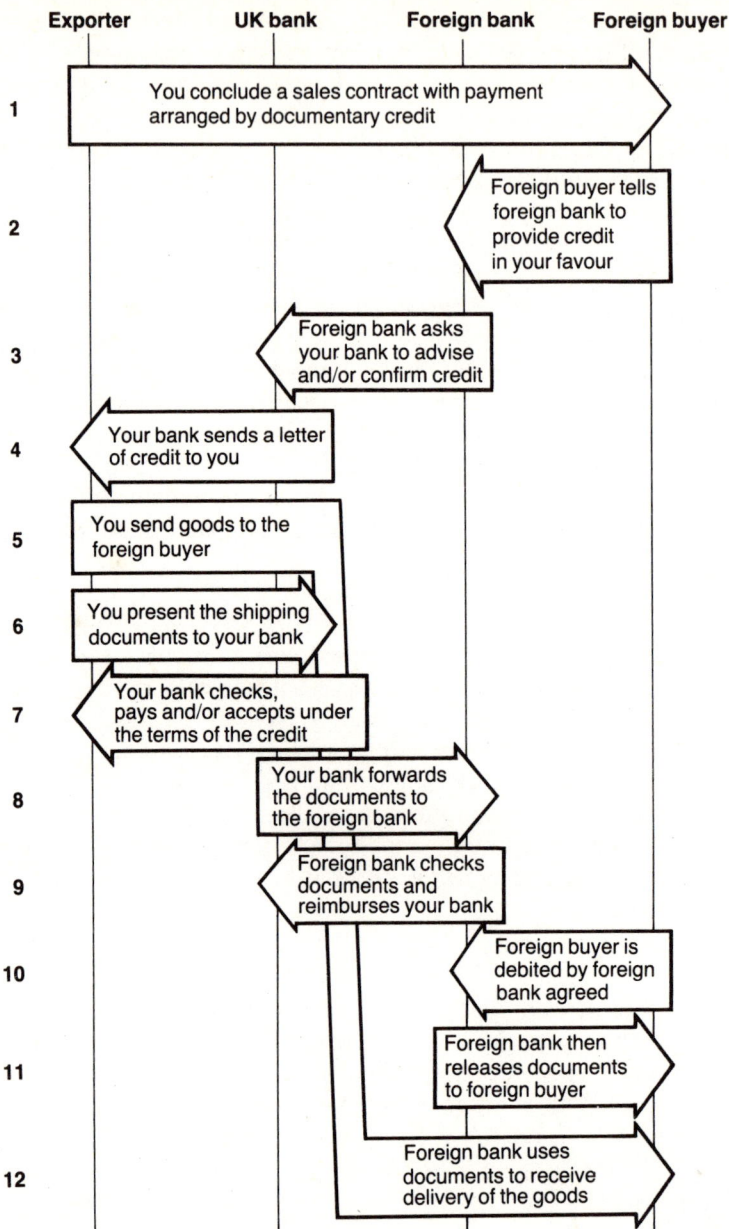

	Exporter	UK bank	Foreign bank	Foreign buyer

1. You conclude a sales contract with payment arranged by documentary credit

2. Foreign buyer tells foreign bank to provide credit in your favour

3. Foreign bank asks your bank to advise and/or confirm credit

4. Your bank sends a letter of credit to you

5. You send goods to the foreign buyer

6. You present the shipping documents to your bank

7. Your bank checks, pays and/or accepts under the terms of the credit

8. Your bank forwards the documents to the foreign bank

9. Foreign bank checks documents and reimburses your bank

10. Foreign buyer is debited by foreign bank agreed

11. Foreign bank then releases documents to foreign buyer

12. Foreign bank uses documents to receive delivery of the goods

Figure 8   *Documentary credits: how they work*

specified sum and are available by, say, three months' date or sight drafts on the opening bank. They are then accepted by the opening bank and handed to you, whereupon you can discount them. In this way, you can raise finance by making use of the name of the opening bank as acceptor, and can discount the drafts at good rates.

Forward exchange

When you sell goods abroad you have the option of invoicing in sterling, or in a foreign currency. If quoted in sterling, the buyer will bear the exchange risk. If it is in a foreign currency, you will bear the exchange risk – and beware because exchange rates may alter substantially. You can minimize this risk by using forward foreign exchange markets. Under a forward exchange contract, your bank agrees to buy foreign currency proceeds for sterling at a future date at a rate of exchange specified when the forward contract is made. The important fact is that the exchange rate is fixed when you make the forward exchange contract and any fluctuations after that time will not affect your income adversely when the goods are sold. (See example below.)

You are selling steel bars for £10,000 to an American importer and the order is taken on 1st August and agreed by both parties. Payment will be made in US dollars and delivery will made on 1st November when payment is to be made.

		Rate of $ to £	$	£ equivalent
1st August	1000 steel bars	1.30	13,000	£10,000
1st November	Rate falls to:	1.20		
	US importer pays:		12,000	£9,230

Note: If the deal had been made in sterling, you need not have worried. The amount would have stayed at £10,000. But as the deal was made in US dollars and the exchange rate went against sterling, you got $1000 less or only £9230.

How do you ensure that this does not happen? You sell forward:

1st August Approach your bank and ask to sell forward. The agreed deal was $13,000, so you ask to sell at $13,000 on 1st November when payment is received *at the rate agreed today.*

Once the bank buys forward it matters little whether the US dollar falls or improves; you are safeguarded and are paid the equivalent of £10,000.

1st November You receive the sum of £10,000 after the bank converts the dollars into cash.

Export credits guarantee department (ECGD)

ECGD is an extremely beneficial service which acts as a safety net for all UK exporters. It is a government department responsible to the Secretary of State for Trade and is required to operate an export credit insurance business to support British exports. The schemes it offers are described below.

Comprehensive short-term guarantee
Short-term credit is for a period of up to six months and you are expected to insure all your export business involving credit terms of up to 180 days. However, cover may be agreed for selected markets, provided these comprise a spread of countries acceptable to ECGD and represent a reasonable proportion of your total overseas business. An exporter is insured against the risks of loss arising from:

- Insolvency of the buyer.
- Failure by the buyer to pay within six months of the due date for goods delivered and accepted.
- A general moratorium on external debt by the government of the buyer's country, or by that of a third country through which the payment must be made.
- Any other action by the government of a foreign country which prevents performance of the contract.
- Political events, and economic, legislative or administrative difficulties occurring in other countries, which prevent a delay in the transfer of payments.
- Legal discharge of the debt in the buyer's country but delay in transfer of currency.

- War, civil war, etc., in other countries preventing performance of the contract.
- Cancellation or non-renewal of an export licence, or legal restrictions on exports.

Once a credit limit is granted on a buyer, it is usually revolving: as payments are received, you can grant further credit, bringing outstanding debts up to the value of the approved limit.

Supplemental extended terms guarantee
This scheme offers credit terms in excess of six months where you are selling, say, production engineering goods. It is available only to those holding a comprehensive short-term guarantee. Cover is limited to delivery periods of two years and a credit period of five years.

Supplementary stocks guarantee
A holder of a comprehensive short-term guarantee may adopt this scheme to insure goods held in stock abroad against war between the UK and the country in which the stocks are held, confiscation by an overseas government, and measures preventing the export of goods. Cover does not extend beyond eighteen months from the date of shipment from the UK.

Services guarantee
This scheme covers export earnings from services to overseas clients, provided such services are either performed overseas or, where they are performed in the UK, the benefits are enjoyed overseas by the client. Typical services covered include: technical or professional assistance; refits, conversions, overhauls or repairs of ships or aircraft; hiring arrangements; and the supply of know-how under licence or royalty agreements.

Bonding
A bond is a written instrument issued to a buyer by a bank or insurance company, stating that an exporter will comply with the terms of the contract with a buyer, or the latter will receive compensation for any loss resulting from the exporter's failure to do so.

Open account scheme

Your bank will advance funds to you up to the total value of the invoice against a promissory note issued in favour of the bank, assuming the note does not go over a credit limit agreed when the facility was established. If the overseas buyer defaults and the exporter cannot honour the promissory note, the bank claims from the ECGD, which in turn has recourse to you for the funds.

Lines of credit

The length of credit will vary according to the contract value, although general purpose lines of credit usually range btween two and five years. The ECGD stipulates a minimum contract value which can be as low as £10,000. The finance available under lines of credit is normally 80 to 85 per cent of the contract value. Ten per cent (sometimes less) of each contract price is usually paid direct by an overseas buyer within thirty days of signing the contract, and further direct payments are made on a pro-rata basis according to the value of each shipment to the buyer.

There are other schemes operated by the ECGD, and some banks offer smaller export schemes for situations where you are unable to meet the normal requirements laid out.

Freight forwarding

The simplest way to arrange the dispatch of products abroad is through the services of a freight forwarder. These firms are experienced in transportation and export procedure and know the special requirements of the particular countries to which the goods are consigned. They can advise on and arrange transport, prepare some of the necessary documents and arrange insurance cover. A forwarder can also offer a 'groupage service', whereby small consignments may be grouped with those of other exporters, often resulting in lower freight and other charges.

British Overseas Trade Board export services

There are a number of facilities which may be helpful to you offered by the British Overseas Trade Board (BOTB):

Export Marketing Research Scheme
This is designed to help and encourage UK firms to undertake marketing research overseas as a key part of their export effort. The BOTB employs professional marketing researchers to advise firms on the best methods of conducting research in overseas markets. In approved cases, it pays a substantial part of the cost of research. The report of an assisted project is entirely confidential. Those eligible are exporters or potential exporters whose goods or services are produced in the UK, and priority is given to applicants with little or no previous experience of export marketing research.

The Market Entry Guarantee Scheme
The scheme is designed to help small and medium-sized firms in manufacturing industry deal with the financial risks and problems associated with a venture to develop a new export market. If, by the end of the agreed venture period, sales have not materialized as expected, then no further levy payments are required and both you and the scheme will share the loss. For this guarantee you pay the scheme an annual premium.

Export Intelligence Service
The EIS helps with overseas inquiries for products and services, agents in overseas markets, and early notification of major overseas (and many other) items of information offering new trade opportunities. You advise EIS on the products you wish to export, the information you need and the markets in which you are interested.

Agency Finding Service
The BOTB will search for suitable overseas agents for you. You will be asked to provide details of your requirements. Status reports on the agents suggested are provided at no cost.

Central Office of Information
The COI provides a free publicity service if, for instance, you have new or improved products, processes or services, or have won large export orders, or have achieved record outputs, or are taking part in overseas trade fairs, or are joining outward trade missions.

European Components Services
The aim of ECS is to provide new market outlets for UK

manufacturers of specialized engineering components in the mechanical and electrical fields by bringing potential buyers and suppliers into contact as quickly as possible. If you contact ECS they are willing to prepare technical translations and drawings and seek out pofential suppliers. Quotations received by suppliers are then compared and suitable ones are sent to you for evaluation. Direct contact between you and the supplier may then proceed. The service is free of charge. The countries with which the ECS deals are Belgium, Denmark, Finland, France, Netherlands, Norway, Sweden and West Germany.

Outward Mission Scheme

The purpose of the scheme is to increase exports by encouraging UK business people to visit overseas markets, either to explore and assess the prospects for their goods, or to reinforce their overseas marketing effort. The BOTB, through its Fairs and Promotions branch, provides assistance to groups of business people travelling as a mission sponsored by an approved trade association, chamber of commerce or other appropriate non-profit-making body.

Trade fairs overseas

Under the Joint Venture Scheme, the BOTB provides space and a shell-stand at attractive rates to each firm taking part in a group display of UK products sponsored by an approved trade association, chamber of commerce or similar non-profit-making body at an overseas trade fair. In addition, for events taking place outside Western Europe, the BOTB provides assistance of up to 50 per cent towards each firm's travel costs and towards the cost of returning unsold exhibits to the UK.

Under the British Pavilion Scheme, the BOTB, through its Fairs and Promotions branch, organizes pavilions or sections to house UK firms and exhibits at certain overseas international trade fairs, providing there are enough firms wishing to participate. These events, which are mainly outside Western Europe, are organized when UK firms would have difficulty in staging an effective exhibit if facilities were not provided. Rents are attractive and the BOTB is prepared to reimburse up to 50 per cent of the cost of travel and the return of unsold goods.

194

Conclusion

Although exporting may seem a little complex, there are many organizations which will help you at every step along the way. You never need to feel that you are left on your own. If your plan is put into operation properly, the potential markets and business which could open up to you could be very substantial, because exporting can be very profitable!

Action Guidelines

1   List the items you need to know about foreign markets.

_____

_____

_____

_____

2   Identify those areas where you will get information.

_____

_____

_____

_____

3   By which method do you intend to sell overseas?

_____

_____

_____

_____

4   List the points that are important relating to agents.

_____

_____

_____

_____

5   Revise the section on documentation!

_____

_____

_____

_____

6   Which method of payment would be most suitable for your business?

_____

_____

_____

_____

7   Make certain you understand the importance of:
    (a) A bill of exchange.
    (b) Documentary letters of credit.

_____

_____

_____

_____

8   What is the value of:
    (a) Acceptance credits?
    (b) Forward exchange?

_____

_____

_____

_____

9   Contact ECGD for further details of their insurance.

_____

_____

_____

_____

10 Contact BOTB for literature on their services.

_____

_____

_____

_____

11 Go to your bank and get information on the economic, trading and
    other details relating to foreign countries.

_____

_____

_____

_____

12 Work out the markets/countries you intend to penetrate and how
    you will do it.

_____

_____

9

How to Work Out the Cost of Borrowing, Interest Rates and Deposits

- How are bank charges applied to your account?
- What are commitment fees?
- Can you be charged if you do not use your loan?
- The money market: can it help you to make money?
- Are you better off with abatement allowance?
- What bank services attract commission charges?
- How can you be caught in the cleared balance trap?

If you borrow from relatives or friends, and they let you have the money free on a temporary basis, you are very lucky, because all professional lenders will charge you interest on any sums you borrow. Banks, finance houses and other financial institutions set themselves up to lend money and they expect to make a good return on it. You, like many others, will be paying for the privilege. But that is only the start of a whole series of payments involved.

Fees

Commitment Fees
In addition to interest rates charged on the loan or overdraft it is

198

also the custom to charge commitment fees for loans. These fees are a once-and-for-all fee calculated as a small percentage on the overall facility agreed. A loan of £50,000 might attract a commitment fee of 1 per cent – costing £500. The reason given will probably be that the bank has to commit these funds for your convenience. However, the fee is always negotiable, and you may be able to get it reduced.

Arrangement fees
This is the charge made to compensate the bank manager for the time spent in arranging the facility. This may be much less than the commitment fee and is also negotiable – to the extent that it could be cancelled if you are persuasive enough. Some banks have quoted a charge of 25p for each £100 of loan, with a minimum of £20; others charge as much as 1 per cent of the loan.

The unutilized balance fee
If you delay in taking up the loan, say, two to three months after acceptance, you will be charged a fee at the rate of about 1 per cent per annum. The bank charges this to compensate for lost interest rates on the facility you have not borrowed.

Prepayment fee
This does not apply to overdrafts, but where you wish to repay a loan ahead of the agreed repayment schedule, you will be expected to pay a fee which is usually calculated as three months' interest on the capital amount prepared.

Interest rates

Interest rates charged to borrowers can vary very widely. The rate is affected by the following considerations:

Credit rating of borrower/element of risk
Lenders are usually pessimistic; borrowers are exactly the opposite. The result is that a business with the best repayment record, or the highest credit rating, will pay the lowest rates of interest; those with lower credit ratings will pay higher rates. If you have a record of non-payment you will find it extremely difficult to

arrange any facilities at all. Major companies, such as Shell, Unilever, Marks & Spencer etc., are known as 'blue chips' which indicates that they are very sound and that the risk of failure is negligible. Any lending, therefore, will be offered at relatively low rates of interest. Your business, however, might be considered to attract a high degree of risk, and the interest rate will be set accordingly. Hence, if a 'blue chip' is charged 1 per cent over the bank's base rate, your business may be charged at 4 per cent over base rate.

The amount borrowed

The amount borrowed will have a bearing on the rate – but not much. Some banks charge a premium rating upon high levels of borrowing where perhaps a business customer's overdraft is never less than £75,000. This 'hard core' of £75,000 may be charged at a 0.5 per cent or 1 per cent higher. Hard-core borrowing relates to loans used by a business on a permanent basis. They are usually overdrafts that are never repaid. If the business pays money to the bank to reduce the overdraft, it borrows up to the overdraft limit later in the month.

The repayment time

This is relevant because certain types of loans (for example, medium and long-term) attract a higher rate. Any other loan deals over long periods of time are likely to be more expensive as lenders have no idea how rates will fluctuate in the future, and they want to avoid rate levels working against them. The rate of interest charged will reflect the lender's view of future monetary values and the risk of non-payment. Usually, the longer the borrowing period the higher the rate of interest charged, but short-term problems in the supply of funds may affect the situation.

The purpose of the loan

This is important as the lender may shade the rate a little if the money is going directly to the purchase of business property, rather than to, say, buying a company car for a director. This means that a rate of, say, 13½ per cent charged for a luxury item might be 'shaded' to 13 per cent for a purchase that would help the business progress.

The security offered

The offer of supporting security usually allows for a slightly lower interest rate, as the lender has some support in case of emergency.

Supply/demand for funds

If there is a low demand for funds or an oversupply, rates will tend to be depressed and lenders may be prepared to accept lower returns to persuade businesses to borrow. For example, if business is at a low ebb and stocks are high, a business will sell its stock and repay its overdraft or loan in preference to buying more stock. The demand for money from the banks will fall and, as more liquidity is retained within the financial markets, rates will generally fall.

Interest rate charges

Interest rates are charged by lenders in three different ways:

1 **Margin over base rate**   Each bank publishes a base rate, which is the point at which its charges begin. They do not always coincide with each other, although differences are usually reconciled in a short period of time. Borrowers are charged a percentage margin above the bank's base rate on loans or overdrafts. High quality borrowers may be charged a low rate of less than 1 per cent over base rate; small businesses between 3 and 5 per cent over base rate; while personal borrowing may be as high as 7 per cent over base rate. Changes in base rates affect the interest rate charged to borrowers – the charges are altered if the base rate goes up or down as in the example set out in Table 13.

Table 13

Date	Base rate	Amount charged over base rate	Interest rate paid
1 June	10%	3%	13%
28 August	9%	3%	12%
15 November	11%	3%	14%
28 December	13%	3%	16%

Overdraft rates are charged on a daily basis on the balance borrowed.

Banks will not allow their base rates to fall seriously out of line with the rates paid in the short-term money market. If this was the case, it would be possible for borrowers with large unused overdraft facilities to take up their borrowing to the full and lend it to the short-term market at a profit.

Margin over LIBOR   The London Inter-Bank Offered Rate (LIBOR) represents the daily cost of wholesale deposits of money moving between banks. Large company borrowers looking for good rates will find LIBOR the most competitive. Rates are quoted at a margin over LIBOR rates and, rather than moving on a daily basis in line with the market, the rate is reviewed at fixed three-monthly or six-monthly intervals, called roll-over points, when the rate charged is adjusted to the relevant LIBOR rate on the roll-over day.

What does one do about LIBOR? How can you find out more about it? The only person who can really help you is your bank manager. You will need to ask whether the bank will be willing to lend to you at LIBOR rates and, if so, whether you may be advised of the rates involved. Then you will be able to compare. Generally, LIBOR rates relate to larger companies, but there is no specific reason why they may not be offered to smaller companies. Thereafter, the choice would belong to you.

3   **Fixed rates of interest**   Lenders are not very eager to offer money in this way. Rates can fluctuate violently, and a substantial loan fixed at, say, 11 per cent could be cheap to you and expensive to the lender if rates rose to 15 per cent and stayed there for some time. Of course, they might fall and it would work the other way. Generally, fixed-rate lending is undertaken by finance houses – most of which are subsidiaries of the main banks. An alternative is for lenders to provide variable-rate loans for repayment by fixed instalments. This alters the length of the repayment period to adjust for interest rate variations – it also helps to insulate your cash flow from interest rate fluctuations.

Bank charges

There are few people who consider bank charges as anything but unpleasant. Unfortunately, each business needs at least one bank account in a British or foreign bank, or a financial institution, and that is going to cost money. The main thrust of most complaints is the arbitrary way in which bank charges are imposed, and the indiscriminate way in which good and bad customers are treated alike. Banks avoid publishing tariffs of the charges they make to business customers. They prefer to deal with each customer on merit and a great deal is left to negotiation. Sadly, a small business will have less to negotiate with than a larger one, and a lot less muscle, but a good bank manager may find a route to satisfy honour all round.

There are basically seven different methods of charging business accounts:

1 **Turnover charge** This is expressed in pence per £100 applied to debit turnover: that is, the value of cheques and cash passing through the current account of the business. For example, 12p per £100 on debit turnover of £500,000 in a year would yield bank charges of £600 for the year.

2 **Item charge** This consists of a single charge for each item relating to credits, debits and standing orders. If 9p is the item charge on a business account, then 350 debits and 250 credits in a year would attract bank charges of £54 for the year. If you are a retailer, you may even find charges being made for bags of change given at the bank counter.

3 **A fixed charge** This method involves a predetermined amount which is charged each year or quarter irrespective of account activity or balances passing through the account. In such a case, a quarterly charge of, say, £100 would be made – depending totally on negotiation with your bank manager and the amount of banking activity on the account.

4 **Split turnover charge** This is made up of different rates of charge expressed in pence per £100, which can be applied to various levels of debit turnover: that is, the value of cheques and cash passing through the account of the business. The result could be as follows:
   Charge 5p per £100 on the first £500,000
   Charge 4p per £100 on the next £250,000
   Charge 3p per £100 on everything else in excess

5 **Split item charge**   This charge is used when all debit items attract a specified rate, except standing order payments which are charged at a different rate.

6 **Free unless stipulations are exceeded**   This category covers those accounts conducted free of charge, or free subject to certain stipulations with regard to the balance in the business account and/or the number of entries. However, if the stipulations are exceeded, charges begin to mount.

7 **Alternative charge arrangements**   There may be alternative arrangements made between you and the bank manager which could be a combination of any of the above forms of charging.

The first five methods of charging may all attract a commission abatement allowance in your favour. This relates to credit monies (that is, cash and cleared cheques) which remain on your business current account each year. Banks recognize that it would be more beneficial for you to deposit that sum elsewhere, even for a short time, and they offer you a low rate of interest against it which can only be set off against your bank charges – it abates them. The rate may be, say 4 per cent, or 3 per cent below the deposit account rate on the daily balance of money in your current account.

Commission

One major factor you will learn in business is that you rarely get anything for nothing. Every service arranged by a bank or an institution will attract a charge against your account. The list below identifies the areas which will cost you money every time you use them:

1 **Arrangement fees:**
   Overdrafts
   Loan accounts
   Farm and produce loans
   Professional loans (accountants, solicitors, medical)
   Small firm loans
   Medium-term loans
   Long-term loans
   Venture capital loans

2   **Perfecting security:** commission will be payable on the facilities outlined above for perfecting security.

3   **Interview time:** commission will be charged on the facilities outlined above for interview time.

4   **Money transmission:**
    Cheques collected
    Cheques paid
    Standing orders
    Direct debits
    Credits
    Cash handling
    Returned cheques/stopped cheques

5   **Foreign commission:**
    Foreign exchange
    Travellers cheques sold
    Cheques/bills negotiated
    Cheques/bills collected
    Documentary collection
    Guarantees/indemnities – foreign
    Securities income, e.g. relating to securities held abroad
    Inward bills
    Mail transfers
    Telegraph transfers
    Drafts/limited cheques issued
    Currency loan arrangement fees

6   **Other:**
    Night safes
    Special presentations (cheques)
    Drafts issued
    Telephone transfers
    Status inquiries
    Safe custody
    UK guarantees/indemnities
    Stocks and shares purchases

Commission is normally charged on a quarterly basis but a forecast of the amount will be difficult as much depends on usage of services rather than any percentage arrangements.

Matters for care

Unagreed overdrafts
Never go overdrawn without first asking permission. Bankers become very sensitive when customers take them for granted. You may shrug and reflect that they can do little about it. Wrong! It may affect your relationship and future credit, and you will be charged a penal rate – as much as 7 per cent over the bank's base rate. After all, nothing was agreed so they will take the initiative. In normal circumstances, the bank may have agreed to charge you 3 per cent over base rate. If base rate is 12 per cent, the charge will be 15 per cent. If permission is not asked, you may be charged 7 per cent over base rate or 19 per cent. This is probably higher than your margins on goods sold at that time.

Bouncing cheques
If you issue cheques for amounts in excess of your bank balance, and there is no agreement regarding an overdraft, the cheques may be returned to the persons you gave them to marked 'Refer to drawer' or 'Please represent'. The bank may charge you £5 for each cheque 'bounced' so it is not in your interests to allow it to happen!

Cleared balances
When you pay a cheque into your bank account it will show up on your statement that day and the total balance will be increased by the amount of the cheque (see Table 14).

If you have practically nothing in your account and you draw out the balance of that cheque within the next three days (or longer if paid in on a Thursday or a Friday, or if there is a Bank Holiday), you will have created an unagreed overdraft. Even though cheques are shown credited on your statement, you must wait until they are cleared, that is sent to the branch of the appropriate bank so that the signature can be checked, and to confirm that there is enough money available for the cheque to be paid. This takes at least three days. If you use the funds of an uncleared cheque, the bank's computer will start charging you. The example shown in Table 14 sets out the problem.

Table 14

	Receipts	Payments	Balance
1 May Balance of account			£1000
1 May Cheque for £1500 issued to creditor paid immediately into a bank			
2 May Cheque received and paid immediately into the bank	£1000		£2000
3 May Clearance day for cheque paid by the creditor on 1 May		£1500	£500

The cheque paid in on 2 May is not yet cleared. Technically, the account is overdrawn by £500 – not in credit by £500.

4 May Clearance day for the cheque paid into the account on 2 May.

Although the statement indicates that the account appears to be in perfect order, you will have to pay interest on £500 for one day because the cheque issued was cleared one day before the cheque received was cleared.

Monetary constraints

At most times you can approach a lender with a fair chance of obtaining funds, but there are occasions when the shutters are down and refusal is almost certain. This occurs during a period of economic distress when the government places constraints on all lending to reduce the money supply. In the past it was known as a 'credit squeeze'. No one can tell how long such as 'squeeze' may last, but you should always be prepared for one to arrive. To this end, it is important that you arrange for lines of credit to be available for your business – preferably from more than one source – in case of emergency. But do not feel too smug after having done so, because when the government imposes financial constraints, lenders tend to reduce limits previously agreed – event to the extent of abolishing them. So do take care to ensure that you are not without funds at a critical time. It should be mentioned that such measures are beyond the control of banks and other lenders, but opportunities exist in export markets, for even in such austere times the banks offer loans to support export sales on fixed terms at cheaper rates of interest.

Deposits

There will be times when you have credit monies either permanently or for a temporary period, and you should make them work for you. This means that you need to watch your cash flow very carefully. There may be many occasions when funds are available to you for, say, two or three days, and you should not let opportunities pass by telling yourself that the rewards are too small for such a lot of effort. In effect, if you reduce the amount of credit to those buying your products or services (for example, make them pay after two or three weeks instead of a month) and increase your credit to those you owe money to (for example, six weeks instead of a month), the sum involved could be used to attract a rate of interest on deposit. If it amounted to £10,000 and you could earn 10 per cent per annum, your business would be better off by £1000 at the end of the year. Your investment decision should be based on the following factors.

1 The size of the amounts available.
2 The period for which the cash is available.
3 Whether there is any possibility that the cash may be required prematurely to make unexpected payments.

Funds should be placed with creditworthy borrowers, with the aim of securing the maximum interest possible, consistent with a good level of risk and your liquidity requirements or negotiability. The higher the degree of risk in the short-term investment, the greater should be the interest being offered. And timing is very important. For example, funds placed on a fixed deposit for three months with a local authority or a merchant bank will not normally be repaid before the expiry of the three months. Treasury bills also usually run for three months, but they are easily negotiable; this also applies to negotiable certificates of deposit.

Differences between these investment opportunities are in the rates of interest, the periods to maturity and the risk. In general, the shorter the life of the investment, the lower the interest earned; the riskier the investment, the higher the interest earned.

Bank deposits
Bank deposits are the commonest form of short-term investment. They are easy to undertake and they are extremely liquid – only a

short period of notice is required before the withdrawal of funds. Any amount can be deposited, with no upper or lower limit. The interest on a deposit account is usually not high but the liquidity and convenience of this type of investment make it attractive.

Deposits in the banking sector
These include deposits with acceptance houses, the discount market, and overseas and merchant banks. Money can be placed on call in a current or deposit account, and the money market may play an important role for your business. Arrangements can be made through your bank as follows:

- **Overnight money** This form is literally held overnight for interest and is returned to you the following day.

- **Money at call** You may have funds to invest for a longer period but you are not sure when you will need them back. This money is best placed on a money-at-call basis; you may call for it any day before noon, and the interest paid is more stable than the fluctuating overnight rates.

- **Money at notice** A more rigid variation is notice money – usually confined to two or seven days' notice. You can renegotiate each time the deposit matures, that is, when the term is up.

- **Fixed money** Deposit periods may be a week, a month, two months, three months, and so on – up to five years.

Be careful not to place a deposit for too long a period if you might need the funds earlier. Once you have placed the money for a fixed term the arrangement cannot be broken. You cannot get your money back until the term has elapsed.

Finance houses
Finance houses offer competitive deposit rates and could be the target for your funds, but you should make certain that the timing fits into your schedule. Once again, a contract for a specified period cannot be broken.

Local authorities
Bonds or bills can be purchased with a period of maturity from two

209

days to five years. You should buy a bond with a life span related as closely as possible to that of your surplus funds. The interest rate would be higher for a bond which had a longer period to run to redemption. But local authority bonds have a lower level of liquidity than most of the other investment options, and the market for them is small.

Sterling certificates of deposit
A certificate of deposit is an acknowledgement of a deposit issued by a bank, and it is negotiable. The period of issue is usually for a minimum of three months and a maximum of five years. The rates of interest payable are higher than those on bank bills, and at least equal to those payable on local authority loans and interbank deposits. Therefore, they offer attractive rates of interest to businesses with money available for known periods of time. There is a secondary market in case of emergency in which the certificate can be negotiated.

Certificates of tax deposit (CTDs)
CTDs are interest-bearing certificates which are proof that deposits have been made with the Inland Revenue to be offset against future tax payments.

Deposits can be made at any Inland Revenue collecting office and the certificates can be offset against most types of tax, except PAYE. These include income tax, corporation tax (including ACT), capital gains tax and capital transfer tax. They can be held by individuals and trustees as well as by companies. The minimum deposit is £2000 with additional deposits moving up in £500 steps, with no maximum. Certificates may be cashed – but the penalty interest payment is 2 per cent less.

In general, CTDs are not freely exchangeable monetary instruments as are certificates of deposit and Treasury bills. Their sole purpose is to be offset against a future tax liability. There is no secondary market, so money tied up in this way attracts the interest penalty. However, the Treasury is usually quite generous with the rates provided on CTDs, occasionally adding bonus rates for medium/long-term holders.

Tendering for Treasury bills
Treasury bills are issued by the Bank of England. Every Friday,

tenders are invited for the bills, which are issued in different denominations. London banks, discount houses and brokers are permitted to offer tenders for a minimum amount of £50,000. Companies cannot make direct tenders, but must go through a bank or broker. The amount tendered per cent is published each week in the financial columns of newspapers. The most common maturity date falls 91 days after issue. A bank or broker may tender, say, £98.85 per cent. The difference of £1.15 per cent represents discount which, of course, is the amount of interest to be earned by lending to the government.

There is no reason to believe that you will not find a suitable channel for surplus funds – whether on a temporary or a permanent basis. The most important factors are the level of rates and the timing; you do not want to find that you have funds on deposit but cannot get at them in an emergency.

Long-term borrowing

The suitability of specific kinds of financial facilities to your business is an extremely important factor, but cost must always be taken into account. There are many management techniques designed to work out cost elements over a period of years against alternative actions (discounted cash flow is one such method) but their use – certainly to a small business – may be complicated to handle, especially when small amounts are involved.

Long-term borrowing is needed in particular for long-term projects:

- Purchase of property or property extension.
- Construction of new premises.
- Expansion by acquisition and business purchase.
- New plant and machinery where the life of an asset is likely to be commensurate with the period of a long-term loan.

The benefits are clear to see, as outlined below.

- Finance is stable in that long-term loans are available for a definite period and cannot be recalled as with overdrafts – unless the terms of the contract are negated.
- The loan can be tailored to meet individual requirements in respect of drawdown, repayment, etc.
- Business growth can be planned more exactly.
- Repayments can be budgeted more accurately.

The costs of setting up long-term borrowing are likely to be higher than those charged for other loans, and may amount to 1½ per cent of the amount of the loan. If security for the loan is offered, there will be an additional charge to cover the extra administrative costs, but secured loans attract lower interest rates. The problem for the bank is that, as loans range between ten and twenty years, and interest rates are volatile, how much extra do they need to charge to compensate for rate variations? Hence, long-term loans will be slightly more expensive than others, even though regular repayments are usually scheduled over the total term of the borrowing.

There is one particular problem for your business in that if security against a loan is offered for, say, fifteen years, you cannot ask for it back to use for other borrowing. It is not available to you. However, major projects do need long-term funds and one should not buck the system if the cost is realistic.

An alternative to long-term lending which is available at very low cost involves equity borrowing as outlined in Unit 5, but this concerns other aspects in the development of a business and should be considered in a separate light.

Action Guidelines

1   How much are you prepared to pay for your overdraft and/or loans?

2   Do you really understand margin over base rate? Write it down
    to be sure.

3   Are interest rates likely to go up or down over the next six months –
    year – two years?

4   How will this affect your borrowing?

5   Which kind of bank charge would you prefer?

6   Think again! You need good reasons for your choice. Write them
    down and reconsider!

7   Which services will you use that attract a commission?

8   Have you estimated for bank charges and commission in
    your budget?

_____

_____

9   In view of arrangement and commitment fees, and high interest rates,
    etc., refer back to your original list of relatives, friends and associates
    from whom you might borrow money. List them now!

_____

_____

10 Describe the problems relating to cleared cheques.

_____

_____

11 Do you have any surplus funds at present?

_____

_____

12 Calculate how much you would have to deposit if you adjusted
    credit from creditors and to debtors.

_____

13 Look at the press and magazines for information on rates offered by
    banks, finance houses, local authorities, etc., and write them down.

_____

14 Make sure you are aware of time scales!

_____

15 Go to your bank and ask about money market terms.

_____

_____

List of Useful Addresses

Government aid

Biotechnology Department of Trade and Industry, Biotechnology Unit, Laboratory of the Government Chemist, Stamford St, London SE1 9NQ (tel. 01 928 7900 exts. 601/628

Computer Aided Design Institution of Electrical Engineers, Savoy Place, London WC2R 0BL (tel. 01 240 8159 and 01 240 1871)

Design Advisory Service Design Council, 28 Haymarket, London SW1Y 4SU (tel. 01 839 8000)

Energy Advisory Service Energy Efficiency Office, Thames House South, Millbank, London SW1P 4QJ (tel. 01 211 3347 or 01 211 7074)

English Industrial Estate Corporation Kingsway, Team Valley, Gateshead, Tyne & Wear NE11 0NA (tel. 0632 878941)

Enterprise Zones Department of the Environment, Room P2/102, 2 Marsham St, London SW1P 3EB (tel. 01 212 3434)

Fibre Optics Department of Trade and Industry, Electronic Applications Division, Room 304, Bressenden Place, London SW1E 5DT (tel. 01 213 5816)

Flexible Manufacturing Systems Department of Trade and Industry, MEE 1 Branch, Room 530, Ashdown House, 123 Victoria St, London SW1E 6RB (tel. 01 212 6515)

Industrial Robots Address as for Flexible Manufacturing Systems (tel. 01 212 0724)

Management Advisory Service Production Engineering Research Association (PERA), Melton Mowbray (tel. Melton Mowbray (0664) 64133)

Microelectronics Industry Support Programme Address as for Fibre Optics (tel. 01 213 5836)

Northern Ireland

Industrial Development Board (50 or more employees) IDB House, 64 Chichester St, Belfast BT1 4JX (tel. Belfast (0232) 233233)

Local Enterprise Development Unit (less than 50 employees) Lamont House, Purdy's Lane, Newtownbreda, Belfast BT8 4TB (tel. Belfast (0232) 691031)

Department of Economic Development Re tourism in Northern Ireland (dial the operator and ask for Freefone 2444 or dial Belfast (0232) 63244

215

Quality Assurance Advisory Service Details as for Management Advisory Service

Small Firms Services Dial the Operator and ask for Freefone 2444

Software Products Scheme National Computing Centre Ltd, Oxford Road, Manchester M1 7ED (tel. 061 228 6333)

Technical Enquiry Service Details as for Management Advisory Service

DTI regional offices

England Charles House, 375 Kensington High St, London W14 8QN (tel. 01 603 2060)
Other local offices are located at Nottingham, Newcastle-upon-Tyne, Manchester, Liverpool, Bristol, Birmingham and Leeds

Scottish Economic Planning Department Industrial Development Division, 45 Waterloo Street, Glasgow CT 6AT (tel. 041 248 2855)

Welsh Office Industry Department, Government Buildings, Gabalfa, Cardiff CF4 4YL (tel. 0222 62131)

Northern Ireland Department of Economic Development, Netherleigh, Massey Avenue, Belfast BT4 2JP (tel. 0232 63244)

Development agencies

Scottish Development Agency 120 Bothwell Street, Glasgow G2 7JP (tel. 041 248 2700)

Welsh Development Agency Pearl House, Greyfriars Road, Cardiff CF1 3XX (tel. 0222 371641)

Tourist boards

English Tourist Board 4 Grosvenor Gardens, London SW1W 0DU (tel. 01 730 3400)

Wales Tourist Board Brunel House, 2 Fitzalan Road, Cardiff CF2 1UY (tel. 0222 499909)

Scottish Tourist Board 23 Ravelston Terrace, Edinburgh EH4 3EU (tel. 031 332 2433)

Northern Ireland Tourist Board River House, 48 High Street, Belfast BT1 1DS (tel. 0232 31221)

British Tourist Authority 64 St James's Street, London SW1A 1NF (tel. 01 629 9191)

CoSIRA 141 Castle Street, Salisbury, Wiltshire (tel. Salisbury (0722) 336255)

Venture capital

British Venture Capital Association Leith House, 47–57 Gresham St, London EC2V 7EH (tel. 01 606 8513)

Ready-made companies

Express Company Registrations Ltd Epworth House, City Road, London EC1Y 1AA (tel. 01 628 5434)

ICC Information Group Ltd 38–42 Banner St, London EC1Y 8QE (tel. 01 253 0063)

Jordan & Sons Ltd Jordan House, 47 Brunswick Place, London N1 6EE (tel. 01 253 3030)

Solicitors' Law Stationery Society 70–74 City Road, London EC1Y 2DQ (tel. 01 253 0444)

Index